MW00779644

LOVE IS THE WAY

Ten Steps to Discovering Personal Happiness

Dr. Michael B. Brown

DEDICATION

To our kids and granddaughter: Adam,
Alison, Andy, Katharine, Zachary
and little Anderson, all of whom help me
understand this topic

CONNECT WITH DR. BROWN

For booking inquires and to join
Dr. Brown's mailing list visit

www.drmichaelbbrown.com

Follow Dr. Brown on Social Media!

@drmichaelbbrown

DR. MICHAEL B. BROWN

TABLE OF CONTENTS

CHAPTER EIGHT:

CHAPTER NINE:

CHAPTER TEN:

INTRODUCTION

We all want to be happy, successful, and fully and truly alive. We sometimes think other people have found the secret to these things, but we're unable to find it for ourselves. Perhaps we followed the detox diets, listened to the gurus' tapes, watched the late-night infomercials, experimented with faith, held hands with greed or sexuality without license, and yet, there's still a gnawing sense inside that something is missing. I reiterate: We want to be happy, successful, and fully and truly alive, but we don't know how.

This book will seek to provide clear and simple answers to the question, "How?" How do I discover a life worth living? Note, the word used is "simple," not "simplistic." There's a difference. Discovering what we desire most in life is not that difficult a task. Rather, the difficulty comes from doing what it takes to achieve it, as that often requires a radical shift in how we previously conducted our life's business. If you're ready to explore that, keep reading.

～～～

In 1998, a man whom I consider one of the two or three greatest motivational speakers of the twentieth century died. Leo Buscaglia helped Americans understand the underlying principle that results in happiness and peace in a way unlike any motivator before or since. His message was simple: Find love, find life! It was not, however, simplistic. Building your life on the principle of active loving is perhaps the most difficult task imaginable because not everyone makes loving easy. It is not always simple even to love ourselves, let alone someone whose sole intent appears to be making the rest of the world miserable. And yet, Buscaglia's message resonated with his audiences in a way that was nothing short of magical. That, I think, is because most of us (whether consciously or subconsciously) recognize truth when we hear it. Buscaglia's truth did not, of course, originate with him. It is the same truth proclaimed by the heroes of all the world's great faiths, the same truth that most frequently appears in the world's lasting poetry and drama, the same truth that quickens or breaks the hearts of those who have experienced it. There is no force so powerful as authentic love. That being the case, there is no life so meaningful as one born of and rooted in that force.

Seated at a table next to mine in a Manhattan restaurant was a thirty-something couple. As our proximity made it impossible not to hear at least some of what they were saying, I was intrigued when the young man concluded their discussion of a troubling event in the current news.

He said, "That sort of thing happens all the time. It's sad, to be sure, but I'm just one person. And what can one person really do to make a difference in a world like this?" Not having been invited to participate in their conversation, and not wanting to appear to be eavesdropping, I resisted the temptation to respond. But had I been invited, I would have replied, "One person can love. That is exactly what one person can do, and one person's love will make a dent in the world's armor. Then, if someone else is inspired by what they witnessed, they will make a dent as well, inspiring another and another until at last the armor cracks and the world can actually be transformed. Furthermore," I would've added, "by the very act of loving, the frustration and resignation I hear in your voice can be replaced by meaning and joy." That is what I suppose I should have said, whether or not I was invited to do so. Perhaps I can still speak the truth to him, if by chance he reads this book. What you and I can do (and are equipped to do, even within mortal limitations) is to love. That much we can accomplish if we are willing to do the disciplined work required. Love has the capacity to change things … to change people … to change each of us. By living lives based on the principle of active loving, we arrive at inner places of peace, positivity, and meaning that all the great motivators of the ages have hoped for their listeners.

～～～

Over years of living and wearing a variety of hats— from preacher to motivational speaker to counselor to professor to friend to spouse to parent—I've consistently observed that those who love the most live the best. It is an undeniable principle of life. By that, I do not mean soft, syrupy sentimentality. Instead, I mean real, raw, down-in-the-trenches love that sometimes defies logic. Imagine if individuals were to make the following single commitment: "From this day forward, I will base all my relationships and all my interactions with neighbors and all my treatment of self simply on the principle of love." What would be the ramifications of that one statement as it applies to global issues, local communities, social systems, institutions, families, relationships, or self-understanding? Life as we know it would be transformed if we finally began not merely to acknowledge but also to practice the truth that love is what life is all about.

Jesus, a wise Jewish Rabbi, reminded his audience of the teachings of the Torah (found in Leviticus and Deuteronomy) that love is at the heart of authentic living. He said that in order to find life, we are called upon to "love the Lord your God, and ... love your neighbor as yourself." (Mark 12:30-31) All the great faiths of the world have used similar language to state the same principle. All the compassionate humanists of the ages have done the same. In short, the great minds of the centuries have been telling us since the genesis of recorded history that whatever else we might have, without love we are impoverished. Likewise, they have reminded us *ad infinitum* that whatever else we may lack, when we find love, we find life.

In this book, I will provide a framework for living based on that historic and too often ignored premise. It will not be sentimental but rather, I hope, practical and helpful. Love is not about sweet songs, soft sonnets, or sugary cards. It can be demanding and exacting. It is both intellectual and spiritual. It involves challenges and changes to one's daily way of doing business. In the '90s, one of the phrases quoted *ad nauseam* in virtually every meeting or gathering was "a personal paradigm shift," meaning a fundamental change in the way a person or group does business. Whether or not you could count on anything else, when going into a meeting in the '90s you could always be sure you would hear that phrase at least once. The '90s (and the century in which they resided) are gone, but the phrase is worth retaining. To build a life on the foundation of active loving is about that—a personal paradigm shift. It is not easy, but it assures that life can become enriching to self and neighbor, that it can become meaningful, that its fabric can be woven with depth and joy and hope. To settle for less is to settle for mere existence. Something within us senses that we were made for more than that.

So, join me in considering what I think is the *sine qua non*, the bottom line, the non-negotiable, for discovering a life worth living. Embrace this principle, and life will bring meaning and joy. Ignore this principle, and ultimately whatever else you accomplish or possess will not be enough. I invite you to explore with me the unfailing truth that *Love is the Way*!

Michael B. Brown

ONE

"WHAT THE WORLD NEEDS NOW"

We've known for a long, long time that, more than anything else, what the world truly needs is love. People were discussing it, professing it, saying it, and singing it for centuries before a pop record reiterated the message back in the sixties.[1]

Wars and rumors of war abound. Military action in Afghanistan and genocide in Syria; unrest in Pakistan, Libya, and Nigeria; oppression and suffering in the Sudan, Somalia, and Yemen; nuclear threats associated with North Korea and Iran; the new Russia becoming the old Cold War Russia and trying to dictate the affairs of Europe and the U.S.; shooters attacking innocent victims in public places; rogue police officers caught on film abusing and even murdering people of color; and escalating political

---

[1] David, Hal and Bacharach, Burt, *What The World Needs Now Is Love*, 1965.

vitriol serve as daily reminders that love is not the central force of the world in which we live. So do all the alarming statistics about the abuse of women, children, and the aged, as well as the constant barrage of anger articulated from far-right and far-left commentators on TV, talk radio, and social media. Obviously (and sadly), authentic love is not the guiding principle of our society. Many fear, in fact, that the discipline of loving has been lost in the shuffle, reduced to the arenas of Hollywood and Hallmark cards. Many of the Woodstock generation who clung to the hope that love would prevail have long since tuned out, conceding that the reality of a greed and self-driven worldview was ultimately too strong an opponent to overcome.

Admittedly, countless post-boomers agree that those aging voices who quit believing in the power of love were correct to concede. Violence is commonplace, from Uganda to the West Bank to inner-city ghettos to the comfortable habitats of the very rich. Deadbeat dads and drugged-out moms neglect the vulnerable and set in motion a continuing cycle of human tragedy. *The Stoning of Soraya M.*[2] is not a fantasy, its thesis being replicated daily in countries and cultures the world around. Greed of epidemic proportion paved the way for pied pipers such as Bernie Madoff to swindle billions and significantly contribute to the near-collapse of the global economic community. Human trafficking is a staggering reality. The divorce rate remains near fifty percent. One-third of American adults at any given moment are dealing with depression, and three out of four with loneliness. In short, to borrow Michael Scheuer's book title, some would argue that as a society we seem to be *Marching Toward Hell.*[3]

---

[2] *The Stoning of Soraya M.*, Mpower Pictures, 2008.
[3] Michael Scheuer, *Marching Toward Hell* (New York: Free Press, 2008).

∿

Take, for instance, a husband, father, grandfather and well-known captain of American industry. With a wave of his hand, he could set in motion business decisions that would affect every aspect of our culture and generate billions of dollars for his company. As one might imagine, he had countless hangers-on: acquaintances, business suitors, and people climbing their own ladders who felt that being close to him would hasten their ascent. He had all the things that money can buy, but as it turned out, that was not enough.

One evening, his college-aged granddaughter stopped by the mansion where the business tycoon had lived with his wife for over half a century. The wife was out at one of her numerous, almost nightly, civic engagements. He spent the evening, as usual, alone, accompanied by CNN and expensive bourbon. When the granddaughter entered the house and called his name, there was no response. Climbing the winding staircase to the bedrooms above, she continued calling for him but was met with only silence. When she pushed open his bedroom door, she discovered the lifeless body of her wealthy grandfather, a power player in American industry, stretched out across the bed. On one side of his body lay a pistol. On the other was a handwritten note that simply said, "I would've traded all to have been loved by someone."

The gentleman who told me that story had been a college classmate of the unhappy tycoon who ended his life and left behind the heart-rending note. The man told me of commencement weekend at his undergraduate school many years before. He had sat with a group of fellow graduating classmates as they discussed their dreams for the future. One by one each student responded to the question, "What do you want to do with your life?" Some wanted to marry and begin a family. Some wanted to land the right job. A couple of them desired to backpack through Europe before settling into nine-to-five work. Others, such as the man telling the story, already had plans for graduate school. One young man in the group spoke clearly and with conviction, saying: "I want to make all the money I can, and then I want to make some more." My acquaintance concluded his story by saying, "That young graduating senior succeeded. He became incredibly wealthy. And one night years later, his granddaughter entered a room and found his body and a note upon the bed."

~~~

Greed, of course, is not the only desire that misguides us in our quest for meaning. My older son, a substance abuse counselor, sometimes observes with a touch of dark humor that his job will never be adversely impacted by a weak economy. His statement is sad but true. Consider many of our attempts to find something that is lacking in life (or to escape life's too-often discouraging realities): chemical dependency, obesity, sexual addiction, etc. All indicate the presence of an almost insatiable hunger to find something—anything—that makes life worth living (or, at the very least, less painful). And in many cases, having devoured what we thought would feed that hunger, we feel just as empty inside as we did before and thus seek something else or something more with increased urgency. Consider, for example, the sad saga of prominent athletes, performers (especially those who become exceedingly famous at an early age), or politicians who could not find an adequate sense of self-worth despite almost unparalleled financial or professional success, and whose bright stars were extinguished through uncontrolled self-indulgence.

Here's the bottom line: Happiness is not attained by having more rooms in your house or followers on Twitter or photos in *People* magazine. Rather, at the end of the day, you and I can find happiness only to the extent that we are loved and that we actively love. Those are the keys. Only through the discipline of daily loving can anyone hope to discover deep, personal meaning in and satisfaction with life.

The title of Jude Deveraux's novel says it so succinctly: We all need *Someone to Love*.[4] It is not enough merely to have someone love us. As important as that is (and it is!), to find ultimate meaning and joy, we are wired to make a meaningful contribution to the world. We are designed to love others. Anything less fails to fulfill.

~~~

I knew a man named Larry. He served for years as the CEO of a Fortune 500 company. Then one morning, with no warning, he simply refused to get out of bed. His wife, Sarah, frightened and unsure of what to do, phoned a minister who lived nearby. The minister arrived within a half hour and was taken directly to Larry's bedroom, where he found the CEO lying in a fetal position beneath the covers. Upon asking what was going on, the voice from beneath those covers replied, "I cannot do it anymore. I cannot go back into that building."

"But," the clergyman retorted, "you have to. People are waiting on you, counting on you."

At that point, Larry inched out from beneath the sheets and blankets, sat up, and began to talk: "I put together multimillion-dollar deals all day long. It's not easy. People

---

4 Jude Deveraux, *Someone to Love* (New York: Atria Books, 2007).

have to perform quickly and without error to make it happen, and I'm the best of the best. That's why I run the place. It is successful because I demand that my executives be as capable and as relentless as I am. I snap my fingers, and they jump. I bark an order, and they tremble. I say the word, and they're gone—good people who studied hard and worked hard but one day made a critical mistake. I say the word, and they're gone.

"So," Larry continued, "I am given respect, but it is based on fear. I see it in my employees' eyes when I walk in a room. I can no longer live like this, knowing that everyone is afraid of me the moment they see me approach. I want someone on this planet to respect me without fearing me." With that, the covers went back over his head.

The neighborhood minister was wise. He acted not in that moment as the non-directive client-centered counselor he ordinarily was, but instead provided helpful advice like a caring grandfather. "Larry," he said, "I know exactly what you ought to do. You need to spend some time serving people instead of managing them."

Larry peeked out from under the covers.

"Why don't you volunteer someplace, helping people who cannot help themselves?" the clergyman posed.

By this point Larry was sitting up again, curious but obviously dubious. "How can I do that?" he asked. "I only have so many hours, and they are slammed."

"Larry," the minister answered, "you have the same number of hours every week that the rest of us do: one hundred and sixty-eight. We all choose how to use them."

Upon the recommendation of another friend, Larry began volunteering two hours a week at a local rehab center. He would read to patients, feed them, help bathe them, wheel them into an outdoor courtyard, and sit with them in the sunshine. He reported to his wife and the minister that it was "wonderful to see their faces when I walk in the room. They break into smiles. Some of them can't speak, but I can see the gratitude in their eyes. They need me. And, best of all, not a single one of them is afraid of me."

In time, Larry made good on his original threat. He refused to go back into his office at the firm. He submitted his letter of resignation and immediately assumed a full-time position at the rehab center for twenty percent of the salary he had previously earned. I bumped into Larry and his wife at a restaurant less than a year later. They were sipping wine and gazing at each other like young lovers. Larry said, "I love what I'm doing, and I never have to force myself to get out of bed in the morning."

Sarah held his hand and smiled. Looking at me, she said, "I lost my old husband. But I like this new one better."

Larry found life by learning to give it away, by offering love to and accepting love from others.

~~~

You don't need a PhD to understand the global ramifications of Larry's epiphany. What would happen if individuals and nations moved from power-based or fear-based philosophies of life to one that simply affirmed that love is the better reality? What effect might that have on the hot spots around the globe that strike terror into our hearts every time we pick up the morning news? What difference could it make in North Korea, the Sudan, Israel, Somalia, Syria, Russia, Ferguson, Charleston or wherever we happen to be? What difference would it make vis-à-vis prejudice, hatred, revenge, violence, al-Qaeda, ISIS, or the abuse of the very young, old, and vulnerable? We know the answer to that question without having to be coached. Swords at long last would be beaten into plowshares.

Is it beyond our powers to imagine a world where political leaders possess sufficient courage to practice peace based on love rather than power based on fear? Is it beyond our powers to imagine a world where journalists and voters make a covenant that leaders who do not govern that way will be replaced by other leaders who do?

The pessimist would argue that the likelihood of world leaders embracing a philosophy of love is not only wishful thinking but uninformed thinking. They would contend that things such as competition for land, oil, and religious dominance preclude the possibility of lasting peace. Certainly they would give little credence to the dreams of poets, philosophers, sages, and theologians who have insisted and continue to insist that there is a better way to exist, and a new ideology can be adopted. Carl Jung was correct when he suggested that people take on an air of condescension and "smile at the very thought of the philosopher's answer."[5]

And yet, how do you respond to the reality that those voices and their stated dreams persist and that something within humanity longs to listen? The very fact that the teachings of Jesus, the Buddhas, and Gandhi are still around after all these years, that they remain globally popular,

---

[5]   C.G. Jung, *Modern Man in Search of a Soul* (San Diego: Harcourt, Inc., 1933), p. 231.

attests to a longing within human hearts for something better, deeper, and more peaceful. And if people of all time periods throughout history have hungered for a way of living with greater depth and meaning, then we who have created faulty systems have the power to create new ones. That is simple logic. The management of life is the property of those who are living. If enough of us no longer trust the old systems, new systems can be established. History is filled with illustrations of that truth. What if enough people become sufficiently (and vocally) dissatisfied with systems built on fear and power? What if enough people finally agree on what the world actually needs in order to become a habitable and hospitable place?

You may be saying, "I cannot change the world." Okay, I will grant you that … for now. (Though I contend that you can be part of the movement that can alter the world.) Still, if you cannot change the world, you absolutely can change *your* world. And that may have the unexpected ripple effect of changing much more than just your own private domain.

~~~

Consider the example of a chef I know in Brooklyn, New York. He owns a wonderful Italian restaurant to which people from all over the city flock night after night. A frequent diner at his restaurant asked him if there is a secret formula to his cooking, something that makes his fare tastier and more popular than that of others. He answered that the secret is his mother. She taught him to cook with love. Despite some obvious dismissive or condescending smiles among his listeners, he continued very seriously to explain that his mother was a first-generation immigrant. They didn't have much money growing up but had the best meals of anyone he knew. Mama cooked authentic northern Italian food, the real deal. And he recalled how she used to say, "When I cook, I think of the people who will sit at the table and how much I love them. So, I try to prepare food that will make them happy." Mama's chief ingredient was love—love for the people who would eat her food. When he became an adult and chose to be a chef, the seed Mama had planted in him blossomed. Throughout his whole career, he has imagined the people who would sit at his tables and has tried to prepare food that will make them happy.

His mother had no fantasy of changing the world through what she did in her kitchen. But her main ingredient was love, and that had a profound effect on a little boy who watched her cook. So, all these years later, he passes along to others what he received from her. People drive from all five New York City boroughs to eat at his tables. Their lives are enriched and their spirits are lifted because, when he prepares for them, his main ingredient is love. Each of us can do something to make our corner of the world better and brighter if we live our lives based on the principle of active loving.

～～～

If one way of living has not brought you personal peace or joy, a new way of living can be adopted. Whatever your age or station, you can change your way of doing business, and that will ultimately change your appreciation of the life you live. You can decide to love. You can decide to make that the central, guiding principle of your relationships, the main ingredient in your recipe of life. This is a commitment you can make fresh every morning: "Today I will be motivated first and foremost by the principle of love. Maybe I failed to do that yesterday. I have no idea what tomorrow will bring. But today I will be motivated first and foremost by the principle of love." It is a decision you have the freedom and power to make, and it is a portal to personal happiness.

Our starting thesis, therefore, is that love is the only genuine source of joy, and it is a lifestyle you and I have the freedom and power to embrace. If nations, governments, and political leaders would be wise and bold enough to embrace that principle, our world would be a very different place, devoid of hunger, oppression, and war. But you and I do not have to wait on governments or leaders to discover what we already know. We have the option every day to choose love and thus to choose life. That is our bottom line. And because of that option, life worth living becomes a viable possibility for us.

However, be warned: the decision to practice the discipline of daily loving is not always easy and goes against the grain of much that contemporary society preaches (by which we have been personally conditioned). Living a life of love is exacting and demanding. Sometimes it calls forth from us things we are not inclined to give. It is far easier to settle for counterfcits of love, to sing a few hymns or teary tunes from Broadway, to give a few holiday gifts, to contribute to an occasional charity, to pet the dog, and thus to assume that down deep we are genuinely loving people. To become a true practitioner of loving is considerably more challenging than that. It is far easier, but always unwise, to settle for less.

So, if we know that we need to find life, which is done by practicing love, then the question becomes, "How do we do it?" How can we recognize what real love is and what it demands of us? How we can practice it? And what changes will be required in our lives? From this point on, it is no longer our task to ask what is needed. That has been established. The task, rather, is to explore how to attain it.

American psychiatrist M. Scott Peck wrote, "The common tendency to confuse love with the feeling of love allows people all manner of self-deception."[6] That is our starting place in the mission to find life by finding love. Love is more than a warm and romantic or sentimental and fuzzy feeling. Instead, *real love is fundamentally an action that we take, not merely an emotion we experience.* If that is the case, then there is but one reasonable conclusion: what the world needs now is a VERB! The world does not need deeper attitudes but more determined actions.

∽

Some years ago, during a trip to Jerusalem, I visited the Holocaust Museum. Outside the building stands a statue of a Polish teacher holding his young students in his hands. It was sculpted as a memorial to that teacher who, during World War II, sought to prevent Nazi soldiers from abducting the children in his classroom and deporting them to the gas chambers at Auschwitz and Dachau. Not himself Jewish, he could have walked away to safety. Instead, he stood between his children and the soldiers, defying the intruders, and at last saying, "You cannot take them unless you take me!" And so he was taken, with the children, to his death. Now his life and his love are carved in stone as ongoing reminders that love is an action we take, not just an emotion we experience. How easy it would have been for him to shed tears, to plead, to say, "Do not do this, for

---

6 M. Scott Peck, *The Road Less Traveled* (New York: Simon and Schuster, 1978), p. 119.

I love these children," but then to step aside and merely observe. Instead, he stepped forward in an effort to resist the invaders and to defend the vulnerable ones in his care. He took action, and his action reminds us all these years later that we cannot afford to step aside and observe. He understood that "love" is a verb.

~~~

Dr. Gerald G. Jampolsky, in his book *Love Is Letting Go of Fear*, told of a time when he was an intern on call in the ER of a large and busy hospital. Many medical students, he said, were intensely afraid of contracting whatever disease they had studied in class the preceding week. For him, that week the word that struck fear was tuberculosis (TB). He found the prospect of that disease utterly terrifying.

As fate would have it, the young intern was awakened at 11:30 p.m. and called to the emergency room where a patient was in serious cardio-pulmonary distress. When he arrived, he found a fifty-one-year-old woman who had stopped breathing. She was suffering from cirrhosis of the liver due to alcoholism. She also had chronic TB.

When Dr. Jampolsky reached her, she had just vomited up blood. A clot was stuck in her throat, and she was suffocating. The young doctor removed the clot from her throat with a suction device and then massaged her heart. Still, she was not breathing and had no pulse. Initially unable to get the oxygen machine to work properly, Jampolsky had only two options: to administer mouth-to-mouth resuscitation on a woman with chronic TB or to let the woman die. Quickly he began breathing into her mouth, and within moments she had a stable pulse. He had saved her life.

Returning to his intern's quarters, Jampolsky saw himself in the mirror, in his words, "a bloody mess." He wrote, "All of a sudden it occurred to me that I had not been fearful at any time during the episode. That night I learned that when I was totally absorbed in what I might get (contract), I was immobilized with fear and was a help to no one, but when I was totally absorbed in giving, I felt no fear."[7] In the act of loving another, his own inner life and sense of peace were strengthened.

Stories like that one abound. Tradition teaches that St. Francis was terrified of leprosy. A story often told about him says that one day he rounded a corner and came face-to-face with an impoverished leper. Francis found himself doing the unthinkable. He dismounted his horse, led the leper to a river, bathed his wounds, and gave him the clean, new clothes he had been wearing, taking the leper's rags as his own. In actively loving, he overcame fear. Mother Teresa cradled the dirty and dying in her clean and healthy arms, often professing that she found the presence of God revealed in them. The list of people who intentionally loved those who are not always easy to love and discovered life in the process is endless. It's not about what you feel. It is rather about what you do because (or in spite) of what you feel. As referenced earlier, there is a profound difference between love and the mere feeling (emotion) of love. Essentially, love really is a verb.

～～

I know a man who has achieved modest success as an inspirational speaker and considerable success as an author. Among his rather broad menu of topics is one regarding

---

[7] Gerald Jampolsky, *Love Is Letting Go of Fear* (Berkeley, CA: Celestial Arts, 2004), p. 79.

how to live the life of love. To be fair, his writings on that particular topic are thought-provoking and scholarly. However, his verbal presentations, while competently done, lack the passion that his words possess in print. Finding that curious, and knowing what a gifted speaker he is on other themes, I asked someone who knows him well to explain. He replied that the man is patently unloving. He is competitive with any others in his field, jealous of anyone who achieves success, almost paranoid in personal relationships, and has a lifelong history of declaring war on any and all colleagues whom he presumes to pose a threat to his personal status (which, sooner or later, becomes "all" of his colleagues). Apparently he has condemned himself to a rather isolated and lonely existence. People avoid significant involvement with him because they hear stories of the wounds incurred by others who journeyed there. Though he is a gifted writer, apparently "love" is to him merely a topic. An idea. Subject matter. Not a verb. If love is simply something we think or talk or write about, but not something we practice, then ultimately we do not understand love at all.

Following a lecture I delivered one night on active loving, a woman came forward and asked a question. She asked it gently and thoughtfully, and I could tell it was not an academic exercise for her. It came from a deep, personal place and revealed a raw wound yet to be healed. She asked, "Is it possible to love someone you don't like?"

I answered, "Yes. Sooner or later, it's the only kind of loving we can do." And that is true. No matter what the relationship, there will come moments when you simply do not like the other person. Most of the time those occasions will be "in the moment" and not permanent. They will not represent an ongoing rejection of the person, of his or her essence or worth. But, in that particular moment, you will not like the other person.

An especially genteel individual might respond, "Oh no. It's not that I don't like the other person. Instead, I simply do not like something he did or something she said." Okay, if you need to make that distinction, go for it. The simple truth is that in the midst of an occasion when another person has said or done something that offends you, your disdain for the offense is virtually synonymous with your dislike of the offender. Whether the other person is a spouse or partner, parent or child, employer or employee, next-door neighbor or best friend, there will be occasions when, however briefly, you simply do not like that person. But that does not mean that you fail to love him or her.

"One of the myths prevailing in the folklore of how to live in the modern world is the idea that one cannot love a person if he does not like him."[8] So wrote the late Dr. Bryant Kirkland, who went on to say that whether or not we like another individual, if the ladder begins to sway, we will still hold it for him. Love ultimately is something we do. And we do it whether or not we may feel like it in a specific moment. Otherwise, love is situational, which makes it provisional ("I will love you if...."). If you are seeking my approval, then your behavior is, in fact, crucial. However, my love is not dependent on you. It is mine alone to give or withhold. This is a fine but critical distinction. You and I can choose to love whether or not the other person is lovable in any given moment. And choosing to love is a gift that, at the end of the day, you give to yourself. It is an action that brings inner peace to the giver.

---

[8] Bryant Kirkland, *Living in a Zigzag Age* (Nashville: Abingdon Press, 1972), p. 65.

∽∾

I often recall the bedtime routine our family practiced when I was a child. My mother and father would come into my room, and before the lights were turned off, we would hug and then say to one another, "I love you." Usually it was an easy routine to follow, as I had kind and caring parents. In retrospect, however, I realize that oftentimes I must have made it difficult for them. And, to be honest, occasionally they made it difficult for me. We were, after all, mortals who brought our own limitations and frustrations and fears and fatigue to the family dynamic. There were times when I had failed to do what I'd been asked to do, and there were times when they had said no when I had begged for yes. All that notwithstanding, it was still our practice to conclude each day by actively showing and stating our love for one another. And love is what outlasted any temporary conflicts. Love is my memory of home. That would not be the case had our love been based upon mere emotion or merit. Instead we understood that, at heart, love is an action word—not merely something we felt, but something we did, a sacred commitment we chose to honor.

Active loving, by definition, requires modes of expression. It is, after all, something we do. The various forms this action can take are almost beyond number. Some are dramatic. Others are subtle. But all are important. Living as a nurse in a leper colony is a dramatic expression of loving, while serving as a nurse in an elementary school may not generate quite as many references in *Chicken Soup for the Soul*. However, in the final tally each endeavor is noble. And each is a helpful expression of love.

Following the tragic earthquake in Haiti in 2010, many people journeyed to the shattered island to assist in the cleanup. They performed surgery. They counseled. They physically dug survivors out from under the rubble. They served food and water to long lines of those who were hungry and thirsty. They set up and staffed shelters where the homeless could sleep. They were on the ground, in the trenches, and their stories inspired us as we saw them on TV or read about them in the news. Others could not travel to Haiti. Instead, they made donations. They gave through churches, mosques, synagogues, and social service agencies. Many gave sacrificially, as the earthquake hit during the height of the global financial crisis. The contributions of those who wrote checks were not regularly reported on TV or in the morning papers. However, without their quiet and often selfless contributions, those on the ground in Haiti, those who traveled there to deliver the goods, would have had no goods to deliver. Over and over we see that same principle lived out. Think of the mega storms of 2017 in the U.S. Virgin Islands, Puerto Rico, Mexico, Texas, Florida, etc. In each place some loved by being physically present on work teams while others loved just as authentically by writing checks. Whether an expression of love is dramatic or subtle, it is still vital and sacred.

The questions we should be asking ourselves are: How can I make love happen actively day by day? What things, large or small, can I do that will make the world a better place than if I left those things undone?

Let's create a checklist. Our next chapter suggests one that works for me and, I hope, might prove helpful for you, as well.

A TOP TEN LIST OF
DAILY LOVING

W hen you think of heroic acts of love, what comes to mind? We can all articulate dreams of storming city halls in defense of the poor, of walking away from a lucrative career to devote ourselves to Habitat for Humanity, of traveling the globe to fight AIDS or starvation, of endowing a children's hospital, etc. Such are noble acts of loving, to be sure, and the world's well-being is dependent upon people who have done and continue to do such things.

The simple truth, however, is that most of us will not be able to scale those particular lofty mountains. We lack the resources. We are not wealthy enough to establish foundations. We are not politically powerful enough to write legislation. Our names and faces are not in the daily news.

In spite of these obstacles, each of us is still able to make some contributions that can affect the world's well-being.

And, in fact, the cumulative effect of millions of people making small contributions almost always eclipses the impact made by any single individual. Add your love to the active love of one million or ten million or a billion others, and you will make the world a much healthier and better place.

Additionally, the benefits of daily loving are not only global in nature. Your practice of love may not impact the entire world, but it will have a profound effect on your world. Your life will become better, brighter, happier, healthier, and infinitely more satisfying than it has ever been before. In fact, it will become more meaningful and joy-filled than it could possibly become through living in any other way.

So let's create a different kind of checklist. When you are crafting it, ask yourself, "What are some things I can do every day to adopt a lifestyle of active loving?" I call the following "My Top Ten List of Daily Loving." It is merely a starter kit litany to stimulate your own thinking in your own way.

1) I CAN LISTEN ATTENTIVELY.

Often, when others are speaking, rather than focusing on their words and listening for the meaning and emotion behind them, we're simply formulating what we will say when the speaker stops for air. "You never really listen to me" is a statement frequently made in a variety of relationships and is usually accurate. We tend to talk with more enthusiasm than we listen.

Sometimes, even when we do listen, we become prescriptive. In other words, once the other person has articulated his or her feelings or dilemma, our initial inclination is to say, "Why don't you do this?" or "If it were me, I would do that." Immediately, that sort of response turns the focus of the moment back to us. It's all about my idea of what the other person should do, or my ideas of the steps I would take. It's all about me when, instead, true listening should be an occasion of concern for the other person.

A more helpful approach is to clarify what the other person is actually communicating, thereby assuring that person of being heard and, thus, valued. For example, "Let me make sure I am hearing you correctly. Here's the situation as you described it, and here's how it makes you feel." A prescriptive approach, at most, should begin with a statement such as "What do you think might resolve this?" or "What do you plan to do?" In a society where eighty percent of adults claim to feel lonely, undervalued, and ignored, few actions are more loving (and healing) than simply listening to someone and thereby communicating that their ideas and feelings have merit.

2) I CAN CREATE "OTHER TIME."

Every day, I can intentionally build into my schedule a bit of time, even if only a few minutes, to nurture someone else.

A friend of mine keeps what she calls a "Love List." It is a list of people she knows (or knows about) who are struggling. Some are homebound or hospitalized with illnesses. Some are going through a season of grief. Some have lost jobs. Some have experienced marital difficulties, separation, or divorce. Some are in assisted-care institutions. Some are suffering from depression.

Once a day (usually during her lunch break at work), my friend takes the list out of her purse and makes one phone call. She simply says, "I was thinking about you and wanted to check in and see how you're doing." That's all. Occasionally the other person will reply, "I'm doing better. It was so nice of you to call." Then a brief, chatty, non-specific conversation will follow. Sometimes the other person will be occupied with something else and unable to talk long. Sometimes she simply reaches their answering machine. But in each of those cases, the person on the Love List will know that someone cared, someone made contact, someone held them in her heart.

Often, however, the person answering the phone will begin to talk about whatever they are going through that is difficult or challenging. They will pour out feelings they had been shouldering alone. Not only is it therapeutic for the person receiving the call, it is also an incredibly loving and satisfying experience for my friend who initiates the call. She says that she cannot count the number of times when, as she is about to conclude the conversation, the other person will say, "I feel so much better. You made my day." Once a day, she takes a few minutes to make one phone call to someone who is struggling. It does not require much from her in terms of time. But it makes the world a better, brighter place by bringing hope and healing to those in pain.

"Other Time" may be constructed in various ways. It can be coaching a Little League team, volunteering in a nursing center, or taking fresh-baked cookies to a home touched by illness or grief. Fill in the blank as you will.

～～

I knew a woman some time ago who was confined to her home due to debilitating arthritis. She was well over ninety years old. For many years, she had been a schoolteacher who was also actively involved in civic and church affairs. At last, she could no longer be active. Additionally, she had outlived most of her friends. Thus, her world had been reduced to a small, usually empty, white frame house on a cul-de-sac in a southern mill town.

She had reasons enough, one would think, to spend her time in a pool of self-pity. Instead, she "went to work" every morning by going to the desk in her den, opening that morning's local newspaper, and writing notes. She wrote to individuals she had never met and would never meet—a young mother who had been hospitalized following an accident that killed her husband, a teenaged boy who had just received his Eagle Scout award, a family whose house had burned, a local girl who had just graduated cum laude from her college, families of people whose names appeared in that day's obituary column. Sometimes she received nice notes in return. Sometimes there was no reply. But she didn't do it to receive. She did it simply to make a difference through loving.

On the day of her funeral, the church where she had been a member was packed with people, the crowd spilling out onto the lawn where they listened to the eulogy through open windows. Many of those in attendance had never met that aged widow being laid to rest. But countless numbers of them spoke variations of the same tribute: "In the worst moment of my life, I received a note from her that gave me the courage to move forward." That wise woman had found joy by delivering love through her daily notes to people. Just imagine how much joy many of those people could likewise have found had they decided to express their thanks to her while she was still alive to hear it.

Once a day, even if just for a few brief moments, we can find our own way of practicing "Other Time." Doing so will make both our world and the world in general indescribably kinder places. If you know of someone with a personal need, express comfort or concern. If someone has been there for you in your moments of need, let them know how much they mattered.

3) I CAN PRACTICE RANDOM ACTS OF KINDNESS.

That phrase has become extremely popular over the last couple of decades. Increasing numbers of people are making conscious commitments that every day, they will do something, say something, or give something that (a) is unexpected, (b) is unearned, and (c) in all likelihood will go unreciprocated. Religious communities often refer to that as grace. Secular communities refer to it as graciousness. Whatever your take on spirituality may be, it is increasingly apparent that life (in a global sense) becomes better and brighter when people (in an individual sense) practice random acts of kindness.

~~~

I waited to meet a friend one afternoon in a lovely retro diner. It was designed to look like a place where people would have hung out in the fifties. There was even doo-wop music worthy of *Happy Days* playing on a jukebox. It was a pleasant place to wait for my friend, and I suspected it was the sort of spot that could turn chocolate milkshakes into an art form. So I ordered one. The young lady behind the counter (who was at most twenty years old) said, "I'll call your number when the shake is ready."

When she called my number, I approached the counter with wallet in hand. She looked at me and said, "There's no charge for that."

I answered, "I don't understand. You can't stay in business long by giving away food or drink."

Smiling warmly, she replied, "Once a day, it is my practice to do something nice and unexpected for someone I don't even know. Today, you're the lucky someone. The only payment I ask is that you pass the kindness along to someone else. Now, enjoy the milkshake."

I did. It was rich and thick and creamy. But more than that, it was a symbol of unmerited kindness, which is the best kind of all. And sip by sip, I kept hearing her words: "The only payment I ask is that you pass the kindness along to someone else." Before the day was over, I made a point of doing that. I performed a random act of kindness for another person, hoping that they, too, would pass it along.

Random acts of kindness are quick and easy. The beauty of them is that they become like stones cast into a pool, creating ripples of compassion that reach far beyond where the stone broke the surface. Committing an act like that is something you and I can choose to do every single day. It requires very little effort and has the potential, in a cumulative way, to have a significant and far-reaching impact.

4) I CAN SEPARATE ISSUES FROM INDIVIDUALS.

This is often difficult, as it is our tendency (and understandably so) to confuse a person with what he or she stands for or how he or she acts.

I once supervised a woman whom I found it hard to be around. My internal stress level increased each time she stepped into the room. Most of the time there was no conflict between us, but I was always braced for it (which made uneventful encounters almost as uncomfortable as those in which conflicts occurred). She seemed to carry a large chip on her shoulder most of the time, tended to see every glass as half empty and was ever eager to assure any person on staff why their idea would not work. She was consistently defensive, bordering on being insubordinate. It seemed to me that there were two options at my disposal: I could terminate her employment, or I could simply avoid her and proceed with my work as if she were not there. Not wanting to harm her ultimate professional goals, aware that there were two or three tasks in her portfolio that she truly did well, and sensitive to the fact that she had young children at home to support, I settled on the second option. I would simply avoid her as much as possible and politely tolerate her when avoidance was impossible.

Despite my best efforts to proceed from a get-along-by-avoiding model, ultimately a standoff occurred. She challenged me over an issue that was mine alone to determine. It was as if she wanted to start an altercation. When I stated, "I am your supervisor. I do not choose to fight with you," she answered, "I don't want to fight. I just no longer want to feel invisible!" Suddenly I understood.

Not only had I confused the issues with the individual, I had virtually dismissed the individual in order to avoid the issues. We disagreed about tasks and topics. We had disparate styles of working. We did not understand or appreciate each other's positions on a variety of matters. So, to avoid the conflicts, I avoided her. And she interpreted that to mean that I disapproved of her, not as a worker, but as a person. From that day forward, though we never marched to the beat of the same drummer, we did find a new and healthier way of relating. I spent more time in her presence. I asked more questions. We both sought to find common ground. I tried to separate the individual from the way she performed her tasks.

∼∼∼

An acquaintance of mine, a decidedly liberal journalist, worked for a while with *The Washington Post*. Not unpredictably, she was predisposed to disapprove of President George W. Bush. In fact, as she put it, she simply did not like him as a person … until, that is, she met him. She reported, "To my utter horror, he was charming. He was affable and gracious, and I found myself drawn to him. To this day," she told me, "I disapprove of numbers of the decisions he made; I think he was ill-advised to do much of what he did, and I probably would not vote for him. But, in all honesty, I cannot say that I dislike him anymore. He's the sort of person I would love to have living next door to me."

Similarly, I know a man, a conservative evangelical minister, who had never met a Democrat whom he likes. He wouldn't vote for one if they were running unopposed. For years the name Clinton all but caused smoke to boil out of his ears … until, that is, he met Hillary. "I had watched her on TV," he told me, "and listened to her. I thought she was brash, hard-edged, and offensive. Then I was in her presence for five minutes, and she was warm and witty and obviously sincere and gracious. When our time together ended, something inside me wanted more time just to be around someone as nice as she had been to me."

～～

We can go on and on with anecdotal illustrations of this principle, but there is no need. It is obvious, and it works. When we are able to separate a person's policies, politics, or practices at work from their essence as a human being, we then become able to love people whom we did not think we could like. And remember, love does not mean that two people have to agree on every issue. It means, rather, that they value each other as humans, in spite of the issues.

5) I CAN COMPLIMENT SOMEBODY.

How simple is that?

A man I've known for years is hard on himself and possesses almost no sense of self-worth. Though clearly intelligent and professionally successful, he always seems to be barely hanging onto life by his fingertips. I understand why that is the case, and I hurt for him. He told me of his father, whom he described as "emotionally aloof." He was not abusive, just disengaged. My acquaintance said that when he was a child, he worked hard academically and usually brought home A's (never anything less than a B). He also labored to keep his behavioral record clean, and every report card included notations from teachers about what a pleasure he was to have in class. Each month, his father had to sign the card before it could be returned to the teacher. Every time, his father would read it, sign it, hand it back to his son, and mutter something like, "Not bad." Then he would walk away. "All my life," the man said, "I wanted just one time to hear him acknowledge that I had done well, that he understood how hard I had worked to do so, that he approved of my efforts, and that he approved of me. But those words never came. And when my father died, I grieved for the man I lost, but I also wept for the dad I had always wanted but never knew." We make a lasting difference in the lives of people when we can bring ourselves to do something as simple as offering a compliment, affirming them verbally.

~~~

It does not require much of us to say, "You worked hard this term, and your grades reflect that. I'm proud of you." It does not require much to say, "You did well on this project, and as your employer, I am grateful." It does not require much to say, "You did such a fine job detailing my car that it looks new," or "I really like the way you styled my hair," or "You have been such an attentive waiter. You really know how to make people feel at home," or "You are the most caring doctor. I feel better when you just walk into the room," or "You know, we've been married forty years, and you're prettier now than you were the first time I saw you." It is not difficult to offer a compliment, and the results of that can be long-lasting and even transformational in another person's life.

6) I CAN MAKE SOMEBODY LAUGH.

Humor dispels (or at least ameliorates) stress, anger, depression, fear, and loneliness. Laughter releases endorphins that stimulate physical and emotional health. Laughter even burns calories. As *Reader's Digest* and the Hebrew Torah have long taught, laughter does good, like a medicine.

An acquaintance spent much of his professional life as a geriatric counselor. Most of his clients could not come to his office, so he spent a lot of hours driving from nursing care centers to private homes, where he would sit with and listen to people with aches and fears and the sense of having been passed by or forgotten. He reported that some time after moving into that rather specialized practice, he discovered a pattern. His clients would request humor. In fact, he said, if even once he told a client a joke, that person would almost always greet him on subsequent visits by asking, "Did you bring me a new joke today?"

"After a time," he said, "in some cases I felt as much like a comedian as a counselor, but I realized the therapeutic value of laughter. And it is undeniable that many a truth is told in jest. Often the punch line of a funny story would do two things: it would relax my client, and it would point them toward a specific topic they needed to explore."

✌

Most of us are neither counselors nor comedians. But all of us are in personal relationships with other individuals day by day. It is likely that the majority of those others are living with personal stress, whether apparent or disguised. Whereas laughter may not resolve the sources of people's stress, it can at least help them cope for a moment. As such, to help someone else laugh is a healing and loving action, when appropriate.

7) I CAN SAY, "I'M SORRY."

This requires a certain level of emotional maturity that can be challenging, because apologies necessitate confession.

Admittedly, it is not too difficult to say "I'm sorry" when our offense has been merely to step on someone's foot as we squeezed past them in a movie theater aisle. It is a far more difficult thing to say when the seriousness of the offense escalates or when there is no recourse for undoing the harm that we inflicted.

We've all seen news stories of convicted murderers who turned to the victims' families and made tearful apologies. Often a family member will say, "It is too late," or "It was insincere," or "That doesn't make up for our loss." And those statements and the emotions they reflect are absolutely understandable. However, countless times we have also heard victims' family members say with anger or sadness, "At the very least, he owed us an apology, but he said nothing. If he had just told us he was sorry, maybe we would feel a little more peace."

In far less serious ways, all of us have harmed others at some point. Acknowledging that (which is a large part of what apologies are about) can become a source of peace, both for the one suffering the offense and for the offender. Guilt frequently vanishes simply with the words "I am sorry," if they are uttered sincerely. No one can rewrite history, but we can resolve present bitterness or future antagonism. And offering an apology is often the catalyst toward doing so.

A note of caution: even as I write this, I realize that saying "I'm sorry" on a daily basis is no doubt taking a good thing to a bad extreme. Few of us have made that many mistakes, and creating reasons to feel guilty is counterproductive to good mental and spiritual health. Do not wallow in feelings of how you may have failed others. Most of the time, others probably do not think you have failed them or do not even remember the incident for which you are apologizing (or at the least did not attach the significance to it that you did). Rather, this point in the litany is simply to note that unresolved ill will is a source of stress both to those who were offended and those who did the offending. If you struggle with guilt about misunderstandings with another, then any day is a good day to take the first step toward putting that relationship right. Doing so usually begins with an apology. "I'm sorry" are difficult words to say, but they can be words that lead to healing and ultimately to the restoration of lost love.

8) I CAN CHOOSE TO FORGIVE.

This is the shoe on the other foot. When someone else apologizes, you can accept them at their word and extend resolution. In fact, you have the freedom to do that even when the other person does not apologize. This endeavor, which leads to a definite and discernible type of personal satisfaction and peace, will be explored in more detail in the next chapter. For now, let it be sufficient to note that maintaining or fostering resentments based on past hurts (whether real or imagined) rarely damages the other person but rather, those feelings damage the person who holds onto them.

9) I CAN CHOOSE TO GIVE.

Whether it is to UNICEF; the Red Cross; Habitat for Humanity; our local soup kitchen or homeless shelter; the Boy or Girl Scouts; a project at our church, synagogue, or mosque; relief and cleanup efforts following a natural disaster; or countless other worthy agencies and endeavors, you and I are provided daily with opportunities to give. And those opportunities are means for putting love into action, for making the word a verb.

Giving regularly does not require wealth, just compassion mixed with intelligence. One of my personal indulgences is a large cup of flavored coffee at my favorite coffeehouse each morning. It costs five dollars. For only a bit more, I could purchase an entire bag of coffee and brew it at home for a full week. But part of the joy of my morning ritual is the ambience. I like the experience. I like the look of it, the smell of it, the regular patrons there, and the Great American Songbook music that is always playing (where else can you count on hearing Perry Como, Dinah Washington, Dean Martin, and Ella Fitzgerald every time you visit?).

~~~

In any event, following a recent devastating natural disaster, I made a decision. For one month, I would brew my own coffee at home and donate my five dollars a day to relief efforts. Though our family gave additional monies to the victims, even had we not given more, my small daily gift (alongside similar gifts from others) would have made a difference. And it was manageable. We can choose each day to do what corporations do: to make "matching donations." The difference is that we match ourselves. We can decide daily to contribute to some worthy project the same amount of money that we spend on ourselves for a specific purpose. We can say to ourselves, "Whatever the amount of my check for lunch, I will match with a donation to a helping agency," or "Whatever the cost of my morning newspaper,

I will match through a caring contribution." You and I can choose to give.

It is an irrefutable principle of life that when we give, we receive. The purpose of giving is not to receive in return; otherwise, we have eradicated altruism, which is the DNA of active loving. That being said, however, when we give, we receive. It's the way the world is constructed.

An acquaintance of mine is a social worker at a state institution for people with serious mental and physical developmental disabilities. As a state employee, she makes a decent wage but certainly not a lucrative one. She pays her bills effectively but is not in a position to put a great deal into savings to prepare for a comfortable retirement. Her hours are long and include weekend responsibilities, possibly explaining why she has spent her life without a significant other. Yet she is as positive and peaceful as any person I've ever known.

I asked, "How do you manage to always remain so happy?"

She answered, "I love these children, and they love me. What more could anyone desire?"

When we give, we get back. It really is that simple.

But even if we do not get back, the world does. Every investment of love that I make yields a positive return in someone's life. Whether or not it is in my life doesn't change the reality that when I love, someone else is the better for it. And, as we previously noted about the ripple effect, perhaps that someone will love another, and that person another, until my initial giving touches and transforms lives in limitless fashion.

I can choose to give. Maybe I do not have as much to give as you, nor you as another, but we all have something. And in the giving of that something, love is put into action, and the status of life on planet Earth is elevated.

10) I CAN SAY, "I LOVE YOU."

Remember what I wrote about my nightly bedtime ritual growing up? I still remember it, both intellectually and emotionally. I can still feel the warmth I experienced when my parents spoke those words. I mattered to someone, and that helped me make sense of life. There is astounding power in those three simple words, life-giving and life-transforming power. By simply hearing them and knowing they are sincere, we can cope with just about anything. "I love you" is a phrase with almost magical properties.

I have known far too many people hounded by grief that is slow to heal simply because of delaying what needed to be said or done. They waited too late to show what needed to be shown, to do what needed to be done, or to say what needed to be said. There is never a more appropriate time to say "I love you" than right now. And there is almost never a good reason to put off doing so. Fortunately, I have also known countless people who processed grief effectively. In almost every case, they were able to say, "They always knew how I felt about them." In other words, those individuals expressed love and thus attended to the most critical aspect of any relationship.

People have a hunger to know that they matter. So, if we love someone, if they bring meaning to our lives, if they are a source of comfort and joy, why would we wait to tell them that? It is a small action that provides great benefits.

And in so doing, the words take on deeper meaning for the one who speaks them. When I sincerely articulate that which is in my heart, in hearing my own words I recognize the depth of their meaning.

"Love," the verb, is more than something we feel. It is something we do on a daily basis, and it requires a conscious decision to move beyond the status quo and change our life routines.

So, let's recap. What are some specific things we can do every day that make "love" more than a mere noun? Consider again My Top Ten List of Daily Loving:

1. I can listen attentively.

2. I can create "Other Time."

3. I can practice random acts of kindness.

4. I can separate issues from individuals.

5. I can compliment somebody.

6. I can make someone laugh.

7. I can say, "I'm sorry."

8. I can choose to forgive.

9. I can choose to give.

10. I can say, "I love you."

None of those acts standing alone may change the world. But each can make a positive difference in someone's life. And cumulatively, if enough of us decide daily to do just those ten things, the world will become a different place. Personally, whether or not anyone else ever decides to live that way, if you implement those ten simple acts on a daily basis, you will begin to discover a sense of peace and joy you had not imagined possible. I promise you that. All it takes is the decision to make "love" a verb.

THREE

THE COVENANT
OF LOVE

covenant is a promise that exists between two parties: "This is what you can expect of me, and this is what I can expect of you." A business contract is a kind of covenant. Marriage vows are another kind of covenant. Covenants happen because we do not live in a vacuum; ultimately, we are all related to and dependent upon one another.

Active loving always involves the movement from "me" to "you" to "us." It is the "us" in covenantal fashion that makes love rich, meaningful, and vibrant. To be sure, I may love you in a way that is not reciprocated and vice versa, but love in its fullness is found in relationships.

Such is the nature of friendship, supported by all the old clichés we've used across the years, such as: "A friend is one who loves us not because of ourselves but in spite of ourselves." Or, "A friend takes my hand, even when in good conscience, he cannot take my side." The world is not in short supply of such adages. They point to a demonstrable principle that cannot be denied—that love works best when it is part of the "us."

This is undeniably true, for example, when the topic is romance. It is entirely possible to be in love with someone who does not feel the same way about you. It's hard to make it through adolescence without experiencing that a half-dozen times or more. We call it "unrequited love," which is, in truth, still love. It can include passion and dreams and hopes and fantasies, but ultimately it is unfulfilling because it is not a shared experience. It never moves from "me" to "us."

The strength of the family unit is located in that very word—"unit." A functioning family is more than an assembly of individuals. It is, instead, a merger of people who have a commitment to interconnectedness that is deep and lasting. Whereas a family may not be like a cruise liner (one solid piece of steel flowing in a single, resolute direction), it is at least like a flotilla (a formation of small ships that may be part of a larger fleet), collected individuals all moving in the same direction and under the same flag.

∿

Some time ago, I got to know a family composed of a mother, a father, a fourteen-year-old son and two daughters, ages ten and three. The father, a member of the U.S. Army, was deployed to Iraq for twelve months. In his absence, the son stepped up to the plate and became "the man of the house" (in whatever sense that family chose to interpret the phrase). Prior to leaving for Iraq, the father took the son aside and gave him his assignment. "While I am gone, you're the man in the family. You are to do the things I have always done. If something breaks, you fix it. If the grass is high, you mow it. If your sisters are frightened, you and your mother comfort them. I even want you to get a part-time job on the weekends so you can help out with the bills."

The young man did exactly what his father asked him to do. He assumed the role, to the extent that a fourteen-year-old is able (and probably more so than any child should be expected to do). Then, after a year, his father (who was his hero, his role model, and his best friend) returned. Suddenly there was friction between the two where none had existed before. His father initially passed it off to his son's age, thinking that teenagers are by nature resistant and rebellious. In time, however, both Dad and Mom had an epiphany. Their son had assumed the role that had been assigned to him, "man of the house." He had done what he was supposed to do, which was to take on increased measures of leadership and authority. And he was reluctant to surrender that and return to simply being a child, which to him now meant "subordinate." The son had assumed a role that can only be occupied by one person at a time, and a battle for power followed.

Fortunately, all parties faced the issue honestly and talked it through, finally arriving at a consensus that there are no "subordinate" roles and that all parts of the household are equally vital and valued. The son even confessed that he preferred returning to the unique beauties of childhood, and the father confessed that he also enjoyed knowing that his son was competent and capable and that his opinions would be heard and taken seriously. From there, they decided to move forward in the same direction.

When there are battles for power or position in a house, it destroys the sense of "us." The ships are jockeying for position, as opposed to moving side by side in a flotilla toward the same destination. For families to be families in the fullest sense of the word, there has to be a sense of "us."

~~~

A man decided to search for his birth parents when he was forty-five years old. Adopted as an infant, he had grown up in a loving home and was deeply devoted to his mom and dad. After they were both deceased, and perhaps wanting to fill the void their deaths had left behind, he decided to find his biological parents. When he did so, his birth father was not even remotely interested in meeting or knowing him, nor did he want his family (a wife and several children) to learn that my friend existed. He simply asked my friend not to contact him again. When the man discovered his birth mother, however, the result was quite different. She embraced him, saying that to her it was as if someone who died had returned to life. She shared with him not merely the medical information he requested but countless other stories of her childhood and the past generations of people with whom he shared DNA. She told him of her painful decision, as an unwed teenager, to release her baby for adoption (an act of both loss and love on her part). She told him of his half-siblings and their lives and natures. She asked copious questions about his years growing up and requested photographs. He discovered two people who had given him life, but only one was willing to offer him the gift of family because that gift, in the end, is covenantal. It is about a sense of "us."

~~~

In the workplace, a sense of covenant is vital to the success of the organization. An employee can be primarily interested in salary, benefits, and vacation days. Or she can be primarily interested in lending her talents to the collective skills of the other workers to produce a product of high quality. A winning football team is not an assembly of gifted athletes doing their own things. There are teams like that, and they rarely bring home trophies. Winning teams exist when each athlete buys into the coach's game plan and contributes his individual talent to a higher good and a shared goal. It's not all about the quarterback, however skilled or well-compensated he may be. The center, the offensive tackle, and the defensive safety are also vital to the outcome of the games.

Almost without fail, at the heart of most successful businesses exists a sense of "us," a commonly-embraced mission that is greater than the sum of the individual parts. Despite each individual's desire for advancement and adequate compensation (both perfectly understandable and expected desires), there should also be a shared commitment to the quality of the goods produced and sold. And that commitment forms a covenant among workers: "We will join together to provide the best possible product to the public who counts on us." That means that in what can often be a competitive workplace, there can also be a sense of "the greater good" that draws coworkers together.

Active love is ultimately about relationship. Consider the marriage vows, "to love and to cherish, for better or worse, in sickness and in health, till death do us part." If either party fails to maintain a commitment to that spoken covenant, the other party acting alone cannot compensate for that. The relationship withers, fails, and frequently ends.

Roughly fifty percent of American marriages conclude prior to the death of a spouse. Even if one party wishes to maintain the relationship, such can only be accomplished when both parties work together within a mutually honored covenant.

Love that is relational depends upon covenant. It depends on trust that each party will do what they promised to do, whether in friendship, family, business, or marriage. Yes, we can love someone who does not love us in return. But never is unrequited love comparable to that which is found in a mutually experienced and expressed relationship.

Are there things that persons can do in order to find the joy available in healthy covenantal relationships? Are there how-to's for covenantal loving? The answer is an unequivocal yes. Consider the following tips for success in loving relationships:

1. COMMUNICATE OPENLY AND HONESTLY.

Many relationships are sabotaged by what I call "relational guesstimates." You know a person well enough to somewhat accurately predict their position on an issue and are unfortunately forced to do so due to their reluctance to articulate. Perhaps three times out of four, you guess correctly (based on past interactions). It is the fourth time, and the cumulative effect of multiple fourth times, that ultimately creates a fissure in the relationship that is difficult, and sometimes impossible, to repair. When a confrontation finally occurs and the silent partner at last decides to speak up, often the time for reasonable conversing has long since passed. Instead there ensue accusations, points and angry counterpoints. One person might claim, "You never ask what I want about anything! You just assume you know and take me for granted. You don't care about what I feel or what I need!" Then the other may respond with, "You never share anything of yourself with anyone. How am I supposed to know? You never reveal any emotions at all. You leave every responsibility for every decision to me and then complain if you don't like them!"

Frequently, conflicts are as much about communication skills (or the lack thereof) as they are about the issue at hand. For eons, marriage therapists contended that couples rise or fall based on the following issues: money, family, sex, and career conflicts. Over time, every competent therapist had added a fifth component to the marriage quadrangle: conflicting roles due to women's emergence in the workplace. However, increasingly therapists have re-thought that ancient approach to marital health and dysfunction. Now, almost all seem to be singing the same tune: relationships succeed or fail primarily because of communication skills. When issues arise about money, family, sex, or career conflicts, the partners who overcome, adjust, and move forward are those who can adequately discuss and process those issues together.

As often as I have heard any other phrase from couples diligently seeking to establish a healthy way of communicating (and thus to salvage a relationship), I have heard, "I never knew you felt that way." That is a phrase that should be foreign within a relationship of love. Establish ground rules, whether at the start of a relationship or when trying to re-establish one. And make sure one of those rules is, "We will not make each other guess what we are feeling." Ultimately, no one can successfully joust against a shadow. We must deal with reality in order to find interpersonal connections that are real. So become comfortable with (or work at growing comfortable with) two statements: "What are you feeling about ____?" and "Here is what I am feeling." Real Estate Agents say that it's all about "location, location, location." We know that when it comes to relationships, it's all about "communication, communication, communication."

2. DO NOT TRY TO RE-CREATE THE OTHER IN YOUR OWN IMAGE OR SOMEONE ELSE'S IMAGE.

An amusing TV ad for an insurance company aired some time ago that showed a couple standing beside a wrecked car phoning their agent, who magically appears like a genie from a bottle. When the woman sees that she has the power to conjure up things that are not, she promptly wishes for a more handsome man, whereupon her man is transformed into an archetypal "hunk." He then wishes the same thing aloud, whereupon she is transformed into a voluptuous beauty. The punch line occurs when the woman (still the same person on the inside) chastises the man by saying: "So, this is what you want, is it? I was perfect just the way I was!" I'm not quite certain what it had to do with auto insurance, but it had a lot to do with human nature. Too often we seek to change another person into somebody more appealing or manageable but would passionately resist their efforts to do the same to us. The bottom line is that a loving partner finds the brightest and best qualities within the other person to focus on and affirm.

How many people, upon entering new relationships, are tempted to try to make-over a prospective partner in the image of his mom or her former husband, his fantasy or her dream? On my way through a crowded parking lot, I heard a woman shout at the man standing before her, "I will never be tall or blonde! Get over it!" A friend dealing with her sense of self-worth said to me, "I always felt the need to apologize to my dad that I was not my older brother."

To bring this to a practical level (and what other level is there as we seek to orchestrate our day-to-day lives so as to find peace and fulfillment in them?), the commitment to refrain from seeking to re-create the other person in a new image often requires the following mantra: "I will affirm the good within you."

Admittedly, sometimes that requires a search, as people bury or disfigure their fundamental goodness beneath layers of posturing, for reasons covering everything from a desire for power to a basic instinct of self-defense. However, everyone has a quality that can be affirmed if we are willing to find it. Let me provide two examples (workplace and family unit), trusting that you can fill in your own blanks with numerous others that spring from or pertain to your own experience.

～～～

In the workplace, unless we are a CEO or otherwise directly involved in HR matters, we work with people whom we did not select. Unlike a marriage, romance, or friendship, our coworkers are simply thrust upon us (and vice versa). Most of us spend more of our waking hours with them than we do with family or friends. So finding a way to relate peacefully and positively is in our own best interests, for there is no fundamental personal peace when our workplace feels like a battlefield.

How do we deal with the coworker who is negative, critical, aloof, overbearing, whiny, or manipulative? Two words: honesty and affirmation. When the other person does something offensive or hurtful, be honest. But state your case graciously. An adversarial response is, "Don't speak to me like that! How dare you!" A response with the potential to foster (or build) a relationship is, "The way you just said that was hurtful. We need to discuss this issue, but let's keep in mind the fact that we respect each other." That response puts the issue of what was said or done on the table, but leaves open a door for conflict resolution as opposed to defensiveness.

What's more pertinent to the topic at this point, though, is the other word: affirmation. Rather than seeking to re-create someone into a different being (which, especially in an office, is rarely successfully accomplished by force), find something within them to affirm. Find the other person's good qualities and bring attention to them in a complimentary way.

Let me confess up-front that this is not easy. The other person is someone whose actions you have found to be offensive. At first, your efforts to affirm may feel gimmicky and insincere. However, as noted, everyone has goodness at some level. You are not creating a myth, nor are you attempting to propagate (and even convince yourself of) a lie. You are, rather, finding a legitimate truth and confessing it. At an unexpected moment, it is possible that a dent may be made in the gruff armor of the other by way of a compliment they did not see coming. Some examples are, "You know, I've never told you this, but I've always felt it. I really respect how much you love animals," or "I really admire how diligently you have been taking care of your mom during her recent illness," etc. Any statement that is (a) honest and (b) approving can be effective. By pointing out (and complimenting) another person's attributes, you reinforce them. By consistently entering into conflict with another, you also reinforce that behavior. And by saying, "If only you would do this or that," you send a message to people that they are not valued, and their rebuttal behavior will be even more alienating.

~~~

The parent-child relationship is another in which it is critical to affirm who a person is and resist the temptation of trying to re-create them into somebody different. "I wish you were more like…" is a phrase that every child hears as, "I do not value who you are. I prefer the other person." I cannot count the sessions I've been part of across the years where a parent and child sat in my office and the child said (in Tommy Smothers-like fashion), "You love my brother/my sister more than you do me." Usually the parent looks surprised, even hurt, and answers, "I love you both the same, but he/she has never challenged me the way you do." That simply does not compute to a child. When a child hears, "I never had to beg your sister to do her homework," or "Your brother's teachers never had to phone and embarrass me about his bad behavior," or "Why can't you make good grades like your friend Erin does?" they perceive a comparison/contrast assessment. What they hear is, "Your sister is more cooperative (ergo, I love her more)," or "Your brother is better behaved (ergo, I enjoy him more)," or "Your friend, Erin, is smarter (ergo, I wish she were my daughter)." The parent may not intend those messages, but they are what the child receives.

The key in parenting is to focus on the issue and the individual at hand. If a child is having academic or behavioral difficulties in school, the issue is about those difficulties, and the individual concerned is that child and no one else. Even when providing discipline, to focus solely on the child at hand is to help the child recognize that he or she is a primary, not secondary, focus. And whereas it is easy to remind a sibling (especially a younger sibling) of an older brother's or sister's virtues, the simple fact is that the younger sibling also possesses virtues that are unique.

∼∼∽

When my younger son, Zachary, entered high school, he followed in the footsteps of an older brother, Adam, who had graduated from the same institution. Adam had been an athlete, captain of the cross-country team, a member of the track team, and popular with his teachers. Zachary began early on to display unhappiness with the school. It had been a positive experience for his brother, so we hoped it would also be for him. Thus were both parents increasingly concerned when such did not appear to be the case. Conversations with teachers provided little assistance, as we were told that there was an "adjustment period" that lasted longer for some students entering high school than others.

The epiphany occurred after Zachary, who was also on the cross-country team, placed high in three successive state meets. Suddenly recruiters, who had been attending meets to watch two seniors on the team, were watching Zachary as well. Then came a meet when numerous recruiters were on hand, and far from finishing near the top, he finished in the middle of a pack of fifty runners. Neither his coach nor any of the rest of us understood what had happened. Was he injured? Did he stumble on the course?

When pushed for a response, he sat on the edge of his bed in his room and a flood of emotion came out. "I am sick of being compared to Adam!" He began to talk of how his teachers expected him to be good in the same subjects as his brother had been, even if his interests were in other subjects. Likewise, when recruiters came to see Zachary run, his coach would tell him he was "living up to the legacy of Adam." And, he continued, in various ways we parents had communicated a similar message. So the frustration had all come to an emotional boiling point on the cross-country course when he decided, "The heck with living up to that legacy! If I can't even be complimented for my own speed, I'll hold back." My son confronted me with the truth that he would never be his older brother, but that, in like fashion, his older brother would never be him. Each child possessed unique talents, and Zachary wanted the world to understand that.

I stood in his doorway, not knowing how to respond, and he added one final statement for emphasis. "By the way, neither you nor my coach has noticed. In fact, Adam is the only person who has noticed or mentioned the fact that I am just a sophomore and have already matched his best speed as a senior!" And with that, despite serious pleas and cajoling from several individuals, he quit the team and never competed again. Fortunately, as an adult, he still loves to run, and he does so regularly with his brother. But years ago, he paid a price to teach the adults around him a valuable lesson: Do not try to re-create anyone in someone else's image. Find value within each child; honor whatever individual quality he or she brings to the table. Otherwise, you unintentionally run the serious risk of making a child feel second best.

༄

Do not hesitate to remind children of the covenantal nature of this relationship. Mothers and fathers, too, should be accepted with grace and compassion instead of judgment. If we are to refrain from making a child feel second best vis-à-vis a sibling or friend, it is reasonable to expect similar treatment. There is no need for oversensitivity. Every child will brag about Johnny's dad who took them fishing or Laura's mom who fixes the best brownies on earth. Those remarks do not indicate a dissatisfaction with a child's own parents. However, statements such as, "I wish you were like Johnny's dad," or "I wish I had a mom like Laura's," cross a line that is intentionally hurtful or manipulative, and every parent has a right to kindly call the child on such remarks as soon as they are made.

3. HEALTHY RELATIONSHIPS MAINTAIN A COVENANT TO HONOR A FORWARD FOCUS.

The history of a relationship provides insights and data that can enhance future joys and protect against future mishaps. However, to consistently dwell within the good old world ("how it used to be with us") or the guilty world ("how you hurt me once") is to diminish, if not doom, the prospects of a healthy relational future.

People in significant relationships (whether romantic, family, or professional) should set goals and check in with each other. The corporate world calls it "strategic planning" and "assessment." Ask the following questions:

- Why are we together (romantically, in business, etc.)?

- How can this relationship be mutually beneficial?

- What do we desire out of having an "us"?

- How can mutual needs be stated and supported?

- What do I need from you, what do you need from me, and how can we know if those needs are being effectively addressed?

All those goals, crucial to long-term lasting success, are founded in focusing primarily on the future.

It is one thing to languish in guilt or anger (depending on your perception of who failed in a particular situation); it is quite another to say, "What lessons can I learn from this in order to build a happier and more meaningful future?" The simple truth is that history cannot be undone or rewritten. There are no time machines. Life is not like an amateur round of golf where you get mulligans, or second chances, for bad tee shots. Instead, life is like professional golf. When you make a bad shot, you must evaluate what happened to your stance or swing so that you can avoid making similar shots for the rest of the round.

We build healthy relationships by creating forward-focused covenants. We agree to a basic principle that, although the past will not be ignored, it is the future that will be the focus of our energy and efforts. "Yesterday" is a great song, but is a woefully inadequate basis upon which to build meaningful interpersonal associations.

4. FIND AREAS OF MUTUAL PASSION.

This seems so obvious that one might think it goes without saying, but this covenantal principle cannot be over-stressed. Whether through culinary, sexual, spiritual, political, activist, artistic, historical or some other form of recreational interest, people who wish to maintain strong connections with others must find a common ground where each is passionately invested.

Fixer Upper is one of the most widely-watched shows on HGTV. It is the real-life account of a husband–wife team in Waco, Texas, who help people (usually young couples on limited budgets) purchase houses that appear ready to collapse or be bulldozed. Then they work their magic and turn those houses into virtual showplaces. The stars of the program are Chip and Joanna Gaines, who met as students at Baylor University, married, have parented four children, and work side-by-side in making dreams come true for people. The show reveals almost nothing of Chip and Joanna's individual faith systems, politics, or their philosophies of history, economics, social justice, or human relations. We do not know if they share the same commitments to athletics, music, travel, fashion, or the arts. We do not know if they vote for the same candidates or enjoy similar foods. Perhaps they share countless passions. Perhaps not. But this one thing is clear: through home renovation, they have found a great passion that bonds them together, an endeavor in which they are both undeniably talented, and an activity they enjoy individually and affirm in each other that brings each of them a sense of fulfillment and joy.

∽∽∽

At a fiftieth anniversary dinner, when a wife and husband were toasting each other, she said, "For all these years, we have had almost nothing in common except for our children and golf. But that was enough." Perhaps not everyone would say that is "enough" to bring the sort of meaning most people hope to get from marriages or partnerships, but the statement was true for her. Only she and her husband could determine what was "enough" in their particular marriage. And she said the two areas where they invested mutual passion, which brought them together, were sufficient: children and golf.

Whatever the nature of the relationship, the chances of it enduring increase exponentially when there is a mutual commitment to some specific issue or activity where both sides can invest passion. We do not have to be clones of each other. How dull it would be if that were the requirement for lasting relationships! *Vive la différence!* However, when there are no discernible areas of shared interests, then initial attraction tends to eventually diminish. This is particularly true in the area of romance. Too many couples learn the painful lesson that sexual appetite does not always retain its original sense of urgency. So the question then becomes: What else do we have that keeps us in love, that keeps us emotionally connected? If there is no ready answer to that question, the relationship is in peril. In fact, frequently it is the other passions that feed (and keep alive) the former one.

5. ALLOW SPACE FOR INDIVIDUAL EXPERIENCES.

This is the other and equally important side of the coin for number four. Whereas there are undeniable benefits that come from shared interests, there is also a bond of respect that is established when one partner affirms (without necessarily sharing) the unique interests of the other. A dear friend who loves opera does not share my love for R&B music. He no longer invites me to go with him to a performance of *Rigoletto*, and I no longer ask him to accompany me to a reunion concert with the Drifters and the Tams. Each friend respects the appetites of the other without feeling constrained to adopt them as personal interests.

～～～

A husband and wife of fifty-two years recently talked with me about their approach to making the marriage covenant work. She said, "I give him Sunday afternoon football, and he gives me Thursday evening book club." With a winning (if somewhat wicked) grin, he added, "And we give each other Friday night!" It was a beautiful testimony to what works—allowing space for individual pursuit and making space for mutual intimacy. As long as that is understood up-front in covenantal form, then neither party feels left out or forced to do things that do not feed them individually.

Admittedly, there are times when friends, spouses, partners, parents, and children do things "with" the other "for" the other, and that is an expression of deep caring. How many parents have accompanied a child to see *Frozen* or *Zootopia* not because they longed to see (or enjoyed) those movies but rather because they love the child? That, however, is not an example of covenant. It is an example of gift, or grace, and is thus a meaningful component of authentic loving. "Covenant" is a mutual agreement, a contract of sorts. A healthy part of such a long-term contract is to agree to disagree about individual tastes and/or needs. She gives him Sunday afternoon football, he gives her Thursday evening book club, and that enhances their sense of togetherness come Friday night.

People do not have to do all things together in order to foster togetherness. In the off-Broadway play *The Body Politic*, two political strategists (one a Democrat, the other a Republican) fall in love. They admit on the occasion of their first tryst that their profound differences in some ways make the occasion all the more passionate.[9] Are we not often attracted to people who take us out of our comfort zones? A professional athlete admires a rock singer who admires a poet who admires an actress who admires a political activist who admires the unnoticed blue-collar worker who admires the professional athlete. Often we find attractive in others specific qualities that are different from our own, which can complement and sometimes even challenge us.

I remember a statement from my boyhood minister, the late Dr. Charlie White, who used to say about marriage, "If a husband and wife agree about everything, what's the use in having both of them?" It was funny, but he made a point. Many different herbs and spices make a broth tasty. Thus, to make a healthy covenant of love is to affirm each other's unique strengths without feeling threatened or forced to conform to them. "I encourage you to do your thing. I appreciate your giving me the room to do my thing. And ultimately, all of that only makes our thing stronger."

6. ELIMINATE JEALOUSY AND COMPETITIVENESS.

This is easy to say but not always easy to do. Jealousy, whether in romance, at the job, or in friendships, has the

---

9   Richard Abrons, *The Body Politic*, At Hand Theatre Company, 2011.

potential to kill real love almost as quickly as any other force one can name.

Most often, perhaps, competitiveness is a culprit that strains the fabric of friendships and ultimately causes rifts. Two friends trying to win the attention of the same prospective date, two coworkers attempting to catch the boss's eye and win her approval, two mothers battling to make their daughters the cheerleader captain, two clergy vying for one prestigious pulpit—in each situation, competitiveness (although a natural and unavoidable part of life) can render people irrational and self-absorbed and destroy relationships when taken to an extreme.

Does it truly detract from your sense of self-worth as a human being if another person is awarded a position you desired? His or her ability (or sometimes luck) in no way lessens your value as a person. Pure logic decrees that different people will excel and possess strengths in different areas. Again, *vive la différence*! The temptation, however, when competitiveness is allowed to migrate to a place of illogical extreme, is to do the unreasonable in order to win the contest or achieve the goal. Lying, cheating, or, at the very least, resenting become acceptable. And in the end, friendship is broken, frequently never to be restored. Therefore, a question of merit when crucial decisions have to be made is this: "Whatever course of action I am considering, in the long run, will what I gain be worth what I stand to lose?" Put another way: Is it worth winning a contest if I lose a friend?

Jealousy has equal potential as competitiveness when it comes to undermining relationships. Unmanaged jealousy in romance, for example, is dangerous and deadly. Note: Be sure to put this into context. A measure of jealousy is natural. In fact, it is an indication that one person still longs for the ongoing primary commitment of the other. "I don't care what he or she does or with whom" is not a loving statement. It is, rather, an indication that love no longer exists.

We all long for loyalty, for never having to wonder if we are honored by the person we love. The jealousy that destroys covenantal love is a different animal from that. It is possessive and irrational. It provides no room for multiple, non-threatening loves. Every friend of a friend is seen as a competitor with the potential of taking the other person from us. As such, this sort of jealousy does not reveal love for another person but instead a consuming addiction to self. "In jealousy there is more self-love than love."[10] And, as statistics can confirm, it can be dangerous and deadly.

A friend who is a pastoral counselor reported to me that jealousy (a reaction to a perceived threat to an intimate relationship) is problematic for one-third of the couples he sees in his therapy practice. It may or may not be the primary reason they sought counseling, but it is a significant contributing issue. Though anecdotal, he attested that most of his colleagues report a similar statistic. Extreme jealousy in a romantic relationship may even cause a person to become emotionally or physically abusive.

～～

The American Bar Association (reporting statistics from the Department of Justice) indicates that, "In recent years, an intimate partner killed approximately thirty-three percent of female murder victims and four percent of male

---

10 Francois Duc de la Rochefoucauld, *Maxims* (1665).

murder victims."[11] A clue that irrational jealousy indicates not love but emotional immaturity (and developmental inertia) is reflected in the fact that in one-third of teen dating relationships, some form of physical abuse exists due to feelings of jealousy.[12] Teenagers, obviously, are still developing emotionally, though that in no way excuses abusive behavior. When such behavior is present in people well past their teen years, clearly some measure of clinical emotional or developmental issues exist that have dangerous potential.

At the very least, jealous behavior pushes away the very people whom we wish to draw near. It is self-defeating and creates a negative self-fulfilling prophecy. I recall hearing a woman report about the frequent jealous outbursts she endured from her fiancé. Prior to their relationship, she had been in a long-term romance with her high school sweetheart. Her fiancé was obviously threatened by her former love. He demanded information that was neither healthy to possess nor appropriate to request, and consistently threw it back at her (often in a rage). He had predictable refrains, depending upon the situation: "I'm sorry I'm not rich like Joe was!" "I'm sure Joe must've been a better lover!" "I bet you never picked on Joe about this topic!" "Maybe you'd be happier if you went back to Joe!" In time, his jealousy became toxic. His desire to possess her had the opposite effect, pushing her away little by little. His lack of self-confidence made her less confident in him. So, one night when he said in anger, "Maybe you'd be happier if you went back to Joe," she answered, "Maybe you're right." And that's what she did.

11   Callie Marie Rennison, U.S. Department of Justice, NCJ 197838, *Bureau of Justice Statistics Crime Data Brief: Intimate Partner Violence* (2003).
12   "Jealousy and Love," op. cit.

Excessive jealousy also accuses the other person at the level of morals and values. It does not communicate, "I love you," but rather, "I do not think you are trustworthy." Who can remain in love for long with someone who makes us feel that way? That is an assault on character, which, if allowed to continue, has a cumulative effect that transforms love into resentment.

So, how does one take steps to prevent irrational jealousy or competitiveness from damaging relationships? The answer has to do with establishing and honoring covenant, both with the other person and with oneself. To accomplish such, one might consider employing the following checklist:

When feeling competitive, or especially when feeling jealous, I will seek to determine the source of my feelings.

I will not speak or act before determining the root cause of my uneasiness. For example, I will ask, "Is the threat to this relationship actual, or is a current incident tapping into stored (and unresolved) pain from a previous relationship?" If I'm experiencing competitiveness, before taking action I will ask, "Is the result of this action worth the cost I may have to pay (that is, injury to or the death of a relationship)?"

In every relationship, we will form a covenant of openness. If either person is experiencing feelings of jealousy, we will address those feelings in calm, reasonable dialogue. We will be honest without being accusatory. We will frame our conversations with "I am feeling" statements rather than "How could you?" statements.

Realizing that where there is no trust, there is no love, we will work together at building trust. We will communicate clearly about those things that create or diminish trust within a relationship. And we will create a mutually agreed-upon list. That list will not demand acquiescence by one to the other, but will simply state commonly-shared expectations that each party will honor.

~~~

From time to time, it is important to remind each other of the original covenant (to live in a positive, loving relationship) and to examine the agreed-upon particulars of the covenant that has been established. Ask, "How are we doing keeping our promises to each other?" or "How are we doing in the effort to build a reasonable and manageable relationship (in the home, the office, the classroom, the neighborhood, etc.)?" At logical intervals, covenants between people, upon careful review and assessment, may need to be edited. The point is that ultimately people must know what they can expect from one another. There has to be a basic common denominator of acceptable behavior. No one can honor rules that have never been articulated.

There is one other crucial component of covenantal relationships. It exists because, however devoted we are to our covenants, from time to time we break them. When that happens, a decision must be made about the value of the relationship at hand. Is it worth doing the hard work of repair, or should it be discarded as the parties move on? If relationships that have been damaged are deemed worthy of restoration, then a crucial component that cannot be ignored is the role of forgiveness in keeping love alive. This issue is so important that it deserves a chapter all its own. That being noted, I invite you to turn the page.

FOUR

LOVE AND FORGIVENESS

ot all of the world's great faiths agree about the role or importance of forgiving those who offend us. Some see it as an indispensable act, without which one cannot adhere to that particular faith. Others see it as an important act, but one that is dependent upon a preceding act (such as confession, repentance, apology, or retribution). Humanists also vary in their opinion of the importance of extending mercy to those who have harmed us. Most credible psychotherapists, on the other hand, almost unanimously insist that there is an indissoluble relationship between learning to forgive and achieving personal happiness. The latter is simply impossible to achieve apart from the former.

It is important from the outset to be intelligent about this topic. There is a marked difference between forgiveness and stupidity. The old adage "Fool me once, shame on you;

fool me twice, shame on me," has been around a long time primarily because it is true. There is no virtue in being a doormat. There is nothing particularly redeeming about allowing the same person to abuse us in the same way over and over and over again. No one should sink to that form of martyrdom.

However, there is virtue in learning to let go and move on. In fact, doing so is fundamental to the discovery of happiness and peace. Counselors and physicians frequently warn that unresolved bitterness is incredibly damaging to those who harbor it inside them. It negatively impacts a person's emotions, outlook, work, relationships, and physical health. So, if you offend me, the forgiveness I offer you (even if it was neither requested nor accepted) is actually a gift I give to myself.

The practice of forgiveness begins with the power of perception. Are injuries real or perceived? Do I perceive injurious remarks or deeds to be intentional or unintentional? Do I perceive the offense to be minor (one that can be dismissed without conflict) or major (one that requires active resolution)? Do I feel offended or injured due to an incident about which the other person may not have a similar perception?

∿

Some time ago, my wife and I attended a seminar. Also attending were numerous colleagues I had not seen in several years. It was an occasion I had anticipated with great excitement. On the first full day of activities, my wife and I were entering a bookstore on the retreat campus. Coming out of the store was a colleague of many years. We had not seen each other in quite a while and enjoyed our brief period of "catching up."

Walking beside him was his mother, a ninety-year-old widow who had accompanied her son to the event simply to enjoy a change of scenery and to have some time with him. As I stood chatting with my old friend, his mother looked at me curiously. She narrowed her eyes and studied me, as if she thought she knew me but was not quite sure. It was the look of one who has another's name on the tip of the tongue, but without absolute certainty that it is the right name.

"Are you Michael Brown?" she finally asked.

"Yes, ma'am. That's me," I answered.

The woman studied me a moment longer and then pronounced, "My gosh, you're looking old!"

It is a sobering moment when a nonagenarian comments on the aged nature of one's appearance.

So, what were my options? I could take her observation seriously and feel wounded (or even alarmed). I could spend far too much time worrying about the remark, staring into mirrors, and buying wrinkle-reversing creams. I could retort, "What an insensitive thing to say—especially coming from someone your age!" Or, I could do what I did, which was to reply, "It beats the alternative!" and then laugh about it.

It was an unintended slight from someone who may well have had reduced mental capacities related to some form of dementia, or may have simply reached an age where she could be completely honest without worrying about it. I choose to believe the former. In truth, the moment was more humorous than harmful. My life is filled with far more pressing things to consider. I don't need to invest time and energy pouting about a perceived insult that was never meant to be such. Of course, my attendance at the gym did increase following that incident, so perhaps I should send her a thank-you note!

It is important to determine if an insult or injury is minor and can be easily dismissed or major and requires resolution. Following lectures, I frequently provide the audience with an opportunity for Q&A, inviting them to pose questions in response to what I said. Most of the time, the questions are actually comments. Nine times out of ten, those comments are warm and affirming. However, occasionally someone in the audience will seemingly "take issue" with something I said during the lecture: "Dr. Brown, you said this, but I have always been taught that. I'm not sure I understand what you mean. And, if I do, I'm not sure I agree with it. Can you clarify?"

An acquaintance of mine, a skilled and articulate speaker, decided to incorporate the same practice into his program presentations. He did so only once. During the very first Q&A, it was his perception that several people challenged what he'd said. He perceived that as rejection and even entered into a rather heated exchange with one of the questioners. Afterward, he dismissed any further Q&A experience from his presentations.

What he failed to see is that the questions posed by the audience, or the reactions that may have appeared as counterpoints to the content that was presented, may have been evidence of how engaged they were by the presentation and how they wished to dive deeper into the topic. As such, those questions and comments are, in fact, compliments to the presenter. They indicate that he or she has stirred within the listeners an increased appetite for the topic. How we react to situations is almost always a matter of perception. Sometimes that which generates resentment within us is, in essence, an accolade.

~~~

Oftentimes that which generates resentment is not worth the energy spent in resenting. Would you leave the theater because someone crawling over you to his seat accidentally stepped on your toe and did not say, "Pardon me"? Of course not. Would you refuse to shop at your favorite store because one time a clerk made a mistake and charged you full price for an item that was on sale? Would you divorce your husband because he did a load of laundry and put colors in with whites? Would you give your wife years of silent treatment because one day, in a hurry, she brought the car home with the gas tank empty? We could create an endless list of ridiculous scenarios.

The point is that people who cope with life with any adequate level of maturity understand that momentary frustrations must not be held onto. Not every word, deed, or slight should be long considered or allowed to become a source of pain. Some actions lack sufficient importance or were unintended. In those moments, let go and move on.

On many occasions, the perception of offense is entirely one-sided. In all likelihood, the people whom we remember and resent do not even recall doing or saying anything offensive. We tend to allow people too much shelf space in our emotional pantries, thus empowering the original hurt to continue hurting and thus to keep us captive. And frequently, if the event were mentioned to the offender, he or she would honestly respond by saying, "I don't recall that," or "Really? That's not what I meant at all." Not every memory is worth hanging onto. Not every insult is important enough to worry about. Not every injury was intended. Not every remark on your appearance by a ninety-year-old should be a source of anxiety. Active loving requires learning to release and proceed to more important matters.

Some injuries, however, cannot be summarily brushed aside. In such cases, to do so is a form of repression or denial that results in long-term emotional damage. A good adage to remember is, "That which is buried, grows."

If something is of sufficient emotional merit to cause ongoing unhappiness, then that issue must be addressed. If a hurt was obviously intended, if you or a loved one suffered abuse, if continued psychological distress has resulted, if a formerly beneficial relationship became ruptured, if personal harm or professional damage occurred, or if life became in some way emotionally impaired because of the actions of another, then resolution is required for your mental (and sometimes physical) health to be restored. And resolution is almost always dependent on intentional and calm communication.

In this day of the Internet, many a quarrel is intensified by the use of e-mails, which do not always contribute to calm communication. We tend to find an unnatural and often unhealthy sense of courage when talking through a keyboard. Anyone can be Rambo when typing. The key to conflict resolution is face-to-face communication conducted intelligently and with a consistent goal of a positive outcome. "I'm going to set him straight" rarely accomplishes worthy ends. "I am going to express how I really feel and see if we can work our way through this" is a far healthier approach. Remember—love is not always easy. And "easy" does not always equal "best."

Often a third party (such as a friend, family member, or trained mediator) can be helpful in moving the process of reconciliation forward. I have some close friends who are the parents of twin boys who they expect "were probably arguing in the womb." The boys love each other and possess the intriguing bond often unique to twins. By the same token, they are preteen brothers and, as such, sometimes exert their independence from each other. On those occasions, they are given to impulsiveness and roughhousing. When serious arguments occur, it is the dad's habit to say to his sons, "You guys just work it out." The mother, however, contends that their way of working it out is often a physical fight. So, when arguments arise, her approach is to say, "Let's the three of us sit down together and work it out." As she puts it, "When I'm in the room helping them express themselves and helping them to understand each other, we wind up with fewer chipped teeth and black eyes." A third party can be inestimably helpful in facilitating conversation and understanding and, thus, in building a bridge across a chasm of hostility or hurt.

Forgiveness is not something that just happens. At the end of the day, forgiveness is something we either intentionally decide to engage in or leave undone. Put another way, it is a personal choice, not a mutual covenant. I can choose to forgive whether or not the other person requested or responds to it. It is an act of love, heightened when offered without requirement of penance.

~~~

One of my closest friends is a person whom I unintentionally hurt years ago. He expressed anger, and I retreated, whereupon the relationship ended. For two years I felt guilt, remorse, and sadness at having lost a treasured friend.

One day, the phone rang. On the other end was my old friend's voice. He greeted me with the words, "Do you remember me?"

I laughed, somewhat nervously.

He continued. "Better yet, do you remember us? I do, and I miss us. So, all's forgiven. I think it's time for us to be friends again."

Each of us works harder now at maintaining the friendship through honesty, sensitivity, and laughter, because we understand what we almost lost until forgiveness restored it. I was inexpressibly blessed by his act of forgiving. That gift is one any of us can provide to another.

~~~

Sometimes, though, we are called upon not so much to forgive another as to seek forgiveness or make amends. Damaged relationships are rarely the total responsibility of one party. And seeking forgiveness can be as difficult as making a decision to offer it. It requires a personal honesty that can be painful. It means looking in the mirror and seeing ourselves as we actually have been, acknowledging what we've done or left undone, and realizing whose bruised feelings may have been left in the wake of our words or deeds. That is not an easy thing to do, but sometimes it is required in order for inner peace (whether the other person's or our own) to be achieved.

A friend of mine told of approaching a man whom he had harshly critiqued in a business setting. The meeting had required open and honest dialogue among workers. Friendly debate would have been healthy and helpful. But my friend went considerably past dialogue or debate in his remarks, publicly belittling and embarrassing a colleague in a truly ugly fashion. He was wrestling with some serious issues both at work and at home. In an unfortunate moment, the anger and discomfort he was carrying inside was transferred, making someone else the scapegoat for his bitterness. It spilled out unexpectedly and inappropriately at a person he liked and trusted, someone with whom he'd enjoyed a friendship, someone who had nothing to do with (and no previous knowledge of) my friend's inner pain. The victim didn't see it coming. He had no idea how to respond. The moment was tense and awkward. For over a week afterward, the two men did not speak, but merely avoided each other as much as possible, not even making eye contact when they passed in the hall.

At last, my friend walked into the other man's office and said, "May I have a moment of your time?" The man pointed him toward a chair. My friend began with the words, "I am truly sorry for how I spoke to you in the meeting." Then he explained that his life had been in disarray. It had all hit a boiling point that morning. His pain had spilled out unfairly at a person who was not the source of it. He concluded with the words, "I haven't slept well a single night since I did that to you."

The other man said, "You should have phoned. I haven't slept well, either." And with that conversation, with that apology, began the reconstruction of a valued relationship. In time, the relationship has become stronger and a greater source of mutual trust and support than it ever was before. And neither party is lying awake at night.

∿

Forgiveness is an act of disciplined love, a gift that we offer to or request from another person. It can also be a valuable and crucial gift we give to ourselves. It is undeniable that to bear grudges against others is to inflict self-harm. Without forgiveness, inner peace is virtually impossible to find.

Years ago, a woman told me of her experience in the hospital following surgery. She had checked in for what was considered a "routine" operation with full expectations that she would spend only two nights there before being released. Instead, following surgery, her pain increased, her appetite decreased, she maintained a low-grade fever, and she had virtually no energy at all. Countless tests were run, all with negative results.

One morning her surgeon, while making his rounds, sat on the edge of her bed and began to speak. "I am a good surgeon," he said. "You could've gone to any hospital in the country and not received better care than you have received here. I did my job. I removed from your body that which was making you ill. By now, you should be home, getting ready to return to work. Instead, if anything, you appear even sicker than when we admitted you." He looked her in the eyes and continued. "I did my part. I removed everything a surgeon can remove. But I think there is something else inside you that only you can remove. And until you do, you will not be well." Thereupon he took his clipboard and exited the room.

The woman said her first inclination was to call him back and say, "How dare you speak to me that way?" However, she reported, "Instead of doing that, I simply broke into tears. I sat alone in my hospital room and wept because I knew he had guessed correctly." Many years before, the woman's husband (whom she'd loved and trusted) walked out of her life and married someone else. She had very little warning and was not given a chance to try to salvage her marriage. He simply announced that he was going, and almost that quickly he was gone. "He was the man I thought I would grow old with," she told me. "He was the one I believed in, but he betrayed me. And from that day on, I was never able to get past the anger. I simply managed it. At least, I thought I did. I believed I kept it under control, but that day in the hospital I realized that perhaps it was controlling me."

So the woman sat in her hospital bed that afternoon and wrote a letter to her former husband and his wife. In it she wrote, "I forgive both of you and wish for you a long and happy life." Interpret what happened next however you choose. I am simply reporting. The following day, her fever broke. The day after that, she was released from the hospital. One week later, she was back at work. Perhaps her ultimate step toward physical healing was something neither the surgeon nor anyone else could do for her. She embraced wellness only when she practiced forgiveness.

∽∾

Whether the long-term effect of grudge bearing is physical illness or emotional pain, it is a burden too heavy to carry. It is one we inflict upon ourselves (as we are the only ones who can choose to retain or discard it). By allowing resentment to continue to smolder within us, we

(a) allow the offender ongoing power in our lives that he or she does not deserve, (b) allow the remembered event to transform into one that is possibly perceived to be even more traumatic than it was, (c) allow time that could be joyous to be irretrievably lost, and (d) condemn ourselves to an existence that is more subsistence than celebration. The truly sad thing is that we're the ones who choose either to remain captured by a former event, thus granting our offender the ability to continue hurting us, or to move past the event (and the offender) to renewed life.

There is another kind of forgiveness required in the search for happiness. It is as crucial as that just discussed, and perhaps sometimes even more so. It is the forgiveness of self. Psychologists tell us that guilt is the most debilitating of all human emotions. Like resentment, if unaddressed it will grow, and the negative results will grow in parallel fashion.

~~~

Consider the cases of Amanda and Greg. First, Amanda. She is a fifty-year-old mother of three. Two children are grown. The third is in kindergarten. In the early years of marriage, Amanda and her husband, Tom, struggled financially, as many young couples do when just starting out in life. They were able to sustain themselves when each was employed full-time. However, with the arrival of their first child, Amanda became a part-time employee, thus learning to make frugality an art form. The second child only exacerbated the situation from a dollars-and-cents perspective. That being said, Amanda and Tom were loving parents, devoted spouses, and "managed" life to the best of their abilities.

As the years passed, Tom's professional life was enhanced by a series of well-deserved promotions in the firm. With each promotion came a higher salary. With that came increased responsibility and greater demands on his time. As is often the case in families with an upwardly-mobile spouse, although the bills were no longer difficult to pay, Tom's role as a family member was to a large degree practiced in absentia. Amanda took on the role of homemaker and primary parent. Tom parachuted in for fun times with the family, thus becoming "lover" to his wife and "buddy" to his children but not a full participant in the day-to-day experience of building and maintaining the home.

At last, life arrived at a place for Amanda and Tom where they seemingly could have the best of both worlds. Having attained an executive position, Tom now had sufficient staff to be able to delegate responsibilities he had previously shouldered solo. Thus, the demands on his time decreased while his income actually increased. Tom could be both adequate provider and hands-on family participant. He convinced Amanda that he had felt cheated the first time around and was certain that they had two grown children who had probably felt cheated, too. He had simply not been with them enough. Perhaps out of a desire to recapture that which could not be recaptured, he pressured Amanda to have another child. It was not too late in the game, he argued. They were both still young enough (only in their mid-forties) and seemingly healthy. This time around he could be a full partner in the parenting process. They both loved children. It would be a whole new chapter for them, and it would help redefine their sense of "family" in a much more meaningful and satisfying way.

Amanda was neither enthusiastic about nor particularly opposed to his suggestion. On the one hand, she had looked forward to the measure of freedom that comes when adult children move out. On the other, as the one who had invested herself so significantly in parenting, she had wrestled with the empty nest syndrome. Ultimately, she consented.

Despite concerns about their age, Amanda and Tom had no trouble conceiving. The pregnancy was without complications or significant challenges. A seven-pound healthy baby boy was born. Mother and father were elated. A new era of life had begun for Amanda and Tom. Six months later, while driving to work, Tom suffered a massive heart attack and died in the back of an ambulance on the way to the local hospital.

Amanda plunged headlong into the traditional process of grief, the first component of which is shock. "Oh no! This can't be real. This can't happen. Not now. Not to us." Depending on which author you read, there are between five and ten stages of grief before one reaches resolution (also called "new normal"). Different authors list different stages. However, all agree that two of the stages one must pass through are anger and guilt. Amanda entered the stages in predictable fashion, once the sense of initial shock had done its work. I came to know her when it became obvious to her that she was not passing through the arenas of anger or guilt.

Put simply, Amanda was angry at Tom. Initially, she felt disloyal to him and his memory by articulating such. So she would only say aloud, "I am angry at myself for allowing him to talk me into having another baby at this age."

In one session, she made the very logical step from repression of the obvious to stating it. "I am angry at Tom for talking me into it."

Next? "I am angry at Tom for talking me into having another baby and then abandoning me to rear the child alone."

Then, "I am angry at Tom for putting me in a position where now I have to become the breadwinner and start anew the long journey to financial stability. But unlike the first time around, there is no parent at home to dutifully care for the child while the other parent is earning wages."

And finally, "I am angry at Tom that I will not experience the benefits of this season of life, but only fatigue instead, as I have to do the hard work of a preceding season from which I thought I had graduated."

What was even more difficult and gut-wrenching for Amanda was reaching the point of being able to state an additional truth: "I love my son, but I would not have chosen him of my own free will. He reminds me of his father, and that causes occasional feelings of anger toward Tom that I fear I will someday express toward my child."

Once Amanda gave voice to those raw emotions, she was also able to give voice to the unwelcome visitor they brought with them: guilt. Amanda felt guilty about the negative emotions that she experienced toward a deceased husband and about the displaced anger that occasionally surfaced in her relationship with her toddler son. It was almost impossible for her to clinically address the anger until she was prepared to dispose of the guilt. I chatted with her about the situation and then introduced her to a competent therapist who helped her claim the obvious as her own: no one should feel guilty about feelings.

~~~

Feelings are, in and of themselves, neither good nor bad, neither right nor wrong. As Lawrence Smith wrote, "Feelings are natural, universal and predictable. 'Natural' means that it is normal and right for us as humans to feel."[13] What we do about what we feel does have moral and ethical implications. But mere feelings have neither. So in order to deal with the anger before it translated into actions, Amanda first had to exorcise the demons of guilt. It is all right to feel, whatever the feeling may be. Guilt is unhealthy and precludes our ability to resolve the pain associated with the primary feeling. Amanda's task was to determine how to process the experience of anger, how to put it to bed so she could move forward with life and appropriately love and receive joy from the child whom she would not have chosen but who was nonetheless a reality. Put another way, Amanda not only had to deal with the challenge of forgiving Tom for putting her into a difficult situation, she also had to forgive herself before she could find healing.

Greg is a fifty-one-year-old husband in his second marriage. His first marriage, in which he fathered three children, ended in divorce when his wife found out about the affair he had carried on for several years. He subsequently wed the woman he had been seeing secretly, resulting in two additional children. I first came to know Greg when he visited me to discuss the idea of ending his second marriage and trying to reconcile with his first wife. The idea was filled with potholes obvious to everyone but himself. Among the rather impressive list of reasons why his plan did not seem plausible were the facts that (a) his first wife, though not remarried, was romantically involved with another man; (b) he had two young children at home with his new wife, and

---

[13] Laurence C. Smith, Jr., *The Nature of Human Feelings* (L.C. Smith, Jr., PhD, e-book, www.lcsmithphd.com/TNOHF-Intro.html), Introduction.

he loved them devotedly; and (c) he was genuinely in love with his current wife.

It does not take Maslow or Freud to rather easily discern the issue at hand. Greg had not resolved the guilt associated with his earlier behavior and had subconsciously concluded that things could only be "made right" by returning to that precise nest. Greg could not see the particulars that were obvious to everyone else, as his emotional pain clouded his rational judgment. Those particulars included the facts that his former wife had no desire to reconcile, and, were that to happen, he would be repeating his previous behavior in reverse form (betraying and abandoning yet another family unit). The simple truth is that history cannot be rewritten.

> The Moving Finger writes; and, having writ,
>   Moves on: nor all your Piety nor Wit
>   Shall lure it back to cancel half a Line,
> Nor all your Tears wash out a Word of it.[14]

Greg's issue was guilt that led to a daily emotional state of remorse. He woke in the night thinking of his act of betrayal, how a spouse and children who had depended on him had been, in his words, "summarily dismissed." It must be noted that Greg's children by the first marriage, while certainly experiencing disappointment and a certain amount of anger, did not share his assessment that he had abandoned them. Instead, when asked, they unanimously attested that in most ways he had been a great father, both before and following the end of his first marriage. His first wife conceded that theirs had not been a particularly happy union, that both sides shared responsibility for that, and that, since the divorce, he had been a generous and kind

---

[14]   Edward Fitzgerald, *The Rubaiyat of Omar Khayyam.*

man to the children and to her. Meanwhile, Greg became increasingly unable to provide satisfactory emotional support and romantic love to his current wife, who had no idea what was causing her marriage to seem more empty and less fulfilling by the day. The culprit was guilt. The antidote was self-forgiveness. Greg's long-term happiness, as well as that of many who were emotionally connected to him, became dependent on whether or not he would at last forgive himself for past decisions that could not be undone.

~~~

Guilt is a genuinely crippling human emotion, building barricades that interrupt our journey toward wholeness. Life is finite. We only have so much time. Either we make it joyful or allow it to be painful. The simple truth is that we all make poor choices from time to time. Those choices cannot be reclaimed or refashioned. We cannot turn back the clock. Thus, the critical choice confronting us all is whether we will allow previous regrettable actions to immobilize us or to educate us.

As the old adage asserts, "Wise decisions in the future are often born of poor decisions in the past." Claim your humanity by allowing yourself to be less than perfect. Learn from the poor decisions that all humans, yourself included, sometimes make, so that you will have a stronger apparatus in hand for making future decisions.

Remember, whether you are part of a faith system or you are a humanist who is well-versed in behavioral science (or are a blend of the two), guilt's only purpose is cognitive. It only serves to teach us lessons that we can appropriate for healthier living in the future. Once those lessons have been learned, the ultimate challenge is to let go and move on. Religious people call that action "grace." Therapists call it "self-actualization." Motivational speakers encourage it by using clichés, such as, "Today is the first day of the rest of your life," or "Each new morning is a new start." Call it what you will. Guilt robs you of the future, which is a sacred and finite gift. Make amends, if necessary. Offer apologies. Seek counsel. But listen to the voices of wisdom, whether they come from the religious, psychotherapeutic, or motivational realm. All those voices agree that guilt is the great enemy of joy, and you have the freedom to offer yourself the forgiveness that restores life. Why would you refuse an option like that?

FIVE

NAVIGATING ROMANCE

The word "love" is more frequently used in relation to romance than in any other way. When we think of "loving" or being "in love," romance is the first topic that jumps to mind. And we tend to harbor unrealistic expectations of what romantic love is supposed to do, be, and feel like—even how it is supposed to occur. Poets, lyricists, and playwrights get lots of mileage out of the phrase "love at first sight," even though any of them who have lived long enough realize that falling in love at first sight is about as likely as bumping into a leprechaun or Bigfoot.

The simple truth is that what we read in romance novels is often based as much on fantasy as on reality. When it comes to maintaining a romance, one cannot avoid the hard work of loving. In this chapter, let's consider what that looks like. What do we look for in a romantic relationship?

How do we know if we've found it? And how can we make it last? Allow me to provide some suggestions in response to those questions. Then you can do with them what you choose. Take them to heart. Put them in practice. Or ignore and discard them, and keep searching for leprechauns.

My children almost never ask me questions about romance. Perhaps that is because children never think their parents have ever experienced it. Obviously, we came into the world old. Just as obviously, we lived our lives with a kind of neo-Victorian chastity. No one wants to think of their parents' passions. Even so, on the rare occasions that my children do broach the subject, there are a few pieces of advice I regularly give. I do so because more than anything else, I want my children to be happy. If people are unhappy in romance, it affects virtually every other area of their lives. Therefore, I give my kids the best advice I have to offer. So that is what I will now share with you.

1. FALLING IN LOVE IS ABOUT YOU.

Later on, it will be about the couple, the family, and other things. But initially it is about you. Your needs matter. Your tastes are important. Your emotions are legitimately a primary concern and consideration. In fact, even the appeal, the attraction, the inner rush of falling in love is something you bring to the table. The idea that another person steals our hearts is mostly myth. We own our hearts and choose, albeit often subconsciously, whether or not to give them away.

Falling in love is a power we possess and we employ. It is not bestowed on us from someone else. No one commands, "You will love him," or "You will give your heart to her."

There is no Cupid, no muse of romance shooting arrows into our unwilling souls. Our hearts are, in truth, ours alone to give. To quote Byron Katie: "If love is not coming from the other person, who is it coming from? There's only one person left: you. You gave yourself the experience of love."[15]

So, falling in love is about you. It is about finding another person who brings out the best in you, who fulfills your inner needs, who enhances your sense of life, and who gives you the opportunity to practice the positive power of loving whereby you find wholeness and joy. Therefore, upon entering into a relationship, allow yourself the freedom to ask, "Is this the sort of person who will bring happiness to me?" Determining if such is the case will take time as well as intelligent observation and assessment. No matter how handsome he is or how sexy she is, the first thing to throw out the window is the old myth of love at first sight.

2. PASSION IS A PRIORITY.

Not the only one, to be sure, but an important one. What you find "handsome" or "sexy" is not irrelevant. Falling in love is initially about you, your needs and your tastes, so it is reasonable to say there has to be passion.

Immediately someone might counter, "Not so. My grandmother was a widow for fifteen years and then, at age eighty, met and married a wonderful man. They are as happy as teenagers, but passion is not a component of their lives." I would then say, "Congratulations to your grandmother and her new spouse! I hope they live to be a hundred and spend every day hand-in-hand and smiling." We witness

---

15 Byron Katie, *I Need Your Love — Is That True?* (NY: Three Rivers Press, 2005), pp. 62–3.

those stories frequently, and they are heartwarming and wonderful. I celebrate what Grandma and her new husband have found. However, what they found is not romance. It is companionship. There's a difference. Romance by definition involves passion. It certainly involves much more than just that, but it does not exist without that.

"Does this person appeal to me in a sensual way?" is a legitimate question for individuals to ask when entering a romantic relationship. A potential partner may be successful and a great wage earner. He or she may be the kind of person you are sure would be a model parent and would relate well in social situations. He or she may share your sense of humor and love of the great outdoors and even vote for the same candidates. But beneath it all, is there a sense of romance and desire for the other person? If not, it is a fact of life that those feelings can rarely be manufactured later on. And that can lead to serious and negatively life-transforming experiences.

Romance is not all about the sensual nature of life. But by the same token, sensuality is a reasonable and desirable component of a fulfilling romance. Sexual union at its essence is a beautiful expression of something words cannot adequately articulate. It is a mutual bonding of two individuals in a way that says, "Here is how I love you as I love no other person." As such it is a unifying experience for a couple, without which the partner who is denied sex may understandably feel unloved, unattractive, or, at least, relegated to the realm of friend instead of lover.

"Sexuality is a major part of life and is an extremely important aspect of a primary love relationship. The contributions that an active sexual involvement can make to the physical, emotional, mental, and spiritual well-being of an individual can hardly be over-estimated."[16] Therefore, upon entering into a relationship and realizing that initially it is about you (your wants, your needs, and your emotions), it is both appropriate and healthy to ask, "Do I find this person sexually appealing?"

3. BEAUTY IS ONLY SKIN DEEP.

When growing up, our mothers told us that "beauty's only skin deep, but pretty's through and through." They were correct. Physical attraction is important. However, there must be something more substantial if romance is to last.

Clair, a woman approximately forty years old who'd been married for fifteen years, came to my office to discuss unhappiness at home. Her husband was not unfaithful, nor was he abusive, and sexual appetite and compatibility had never been problems. Still, she seemed deeply dissatisfied with her marriage. After considerable conversation, she blurted out a statement intended to be humorous. Immediately the old saying that "many a truth is said in jest" was proven true. Clair said, "Charlie has always been an indescribably handsome man, and he gets better with age. When I first met him, I was swept away by his blue eyes. They are so blue that they almost shine, like Caribbean waters. But I finally realized that right behind those blue eyes is just empty space." She laughed at her own joke, but then grew silent and pensive. After a moment, she looked at me and said, "My God, that's it! That's what's wrong. I can have sex with him, but I can't have a serious conversation with him. He doesn't read. He doesn't care about current events. He will not go with me to the theater, but I'm

---

16   Hal and Sidra Stone, *Embracing Each Other* (Albion, CA: Delos, Inc., 1989), p. 195.

supposed to go with him on fishing trips. I cannot have an intelligent verbal exchange with my husband. There's just nothing behind those blue eyes."

Beauty is only skin deep, and in time, skin changes. An undeniably important question to ask is, "What will remain when the beauty has faded?" Is the other person someone you like and not merely someone you desire? Are you both compatible in ways that go beyond sexuality? Do you share similar values, tastes, and commitments?

4. IT IS IMPORTANT TO BE FLEXIBLE.

You and your partner do not have to be clones of each other. That is neither desirable nor healthy. You will inevitably have certain tastes that are profoundly different, which is truly okay. Whoever said that compromise is the queen of the virtues was a wise soul. At the beginning of a romantic relationship, it is primarily about you. And that's how it should be. However, as the relationship progresses, it becomes about "us." (Remember the importance of covenant in a loving relationship.)

Flexibility, put simply, means that it is not always "all about me." Charlie was not to be blamed for wanting Clair to go on fishing expeditions with him. However, reasonable flexibility would suggest that he, then, should have been willing to accompany her to the opera. Whereas people may demand activities or responses from other people, what they cannot demand is love. Those who choose to be demanding, controlling, authoritarian, or self-centered in relationships sooner or later manage to eradicate the love that the other person used to feel.

In truth, by participating in (or, at least, exposing ourselves to) activities we do not necessarily enjoy, we grow as intellectual human beings. Page, my wife, was an art major and has a passion for the paintings of the masters. I was a first baseman and have a passion for seeing someone stretch a single into a double. Because of her, I have discovered the joys (and frequent stress relief) of spending an afternoon in a museum. Because of me, she has learned to happily munch on a stadium chili dog while understanding the difference between a fly out and a sacrifice fly. Flexibility and a willingness to participate in a way that brings joy to the other have broadened our own individual scopes of interest.

Flexibility is certainly about more than mere hobbies or activities. It also is about people, specifically the people that someone else brings to the romance. More than once I have witnessed significant difficulties occur in romantic relationships because one partner expected the other to be deeply involved in the life of his or her extended family but resisted doing likewise. The plain truth is that when we enter into a romantic commitment with another person, we enter into whatever world is theirs. And that includes their parents, children, siblings, business associates, and close friends. We do not live in a vacuum. Unless two hermits fall in love and reside forever on a deserted island, people enter into relationships aware that there are significant others (plural) in the universe of that one significant other. And if I expect you to embrace my family and friends, it is patently unfair and immature of me not to extend the same kindness. Furthermore, in time my resistance to those who matter to you coupled with my insistence that you love those dear to me will destroy the romantic love that once existed between us.

5. STAY TRUE TO YOU.

Flexibility is important. As a romance grows, it is no longer all about you, but rather "all about us." And that requires a mutuality of involvement in things either partner may not have chosen before. However, remaining flexible and practicing the compassion of compromise does not mean allowing yourself to be absorbed by the other person. When she was fourteen, our daughter, Katharine, had a momentary epiphany one evening at the dinner table. I don't recall what prompted her comment, but I do remember her words. "I'm never going to give up on being me. I'm just going to try to be the best me that I can." Good decision!

Included in wedding services in some religious traditions is a beautiful liturgical symbol: the lighting of the Unity Candle. Two small, burning candles sit on either side of a large, white, unlit one. The outer candles represent the bride and groom, as well as their families. Following the moment when the couple is pronounced "husband and wife," they step forward together, take flame from the outer candles, and jointly light the center one. It is a symbol of the two becoming one. However, in that liturgy the external candles are not extinguished. They continue to burn individually, on their own. That is a visible reminder that though people come together in relationship, they still retain personality, individuality, and additional emotional bonds. Neither person is intended to be swallowed up by the other.

In healthy romantic relationships, the reality of the individual self is acknowledged and affirmed. One of the most loving couples I know sets aside Friday and Saturday nights as "special evenings." Friday is called "Guys'/Girls' Night Out." Each partner arranges an evening with friends, romantic partners not included. Saturday is called "Date Night." The couple devotes that evening purely to themselves as a couple, children (and usually friends) not included. They nurture the "us" but also affirm in each other the individual "you."

If you are a jogger and your partner does Pilates, there is no reason either of you should give up what works for you physically simply because it is not an activity you enjoy doing together. If you like noir movies and your partner likes rom-coms, there is no reason either of you should give up watching what you enjoy simply because the other person does not share your taste in film. If you love your extended family and cherish time with them, it is unthinkable that you would distance yourself from them because they are not your partner's family—just as it is unthinkable that you would allow your parents or siblings to drive a wedge between you and your partner. "Love" does not equal "absorption." Though it is always important to focus on enhancing a sense of "us," it is not healthy to seek for or demand "only us."

6. "ME TIME" ENHANCES "OUR TIME."

Once I am refreshed or renewed, there is more of me to energetically, lovingly, and passionately share with "the other."

It is to a great extent true that "absence makes the heart grow fonder." Upon his return from extended duty in Afghanistan, a military vet said to me, "I've never loved my family more, or felt more loved by them, than when I came home after that long, lonely absence." Being apart for a while deepens our appreciation of being reunited and, thus, enriches the sense of togetherness that loving partners share.

There is a difference, of course, between consistently "doing my own thing" and occasionally "taking time for self." The former can damage a relationship, making one partner feel ignored or abandoned. The latter, however, can immeasurably strengthen the bond between two people. Speaking from my own perspective as an introvert, from time to time I need solitude. Whatever your Myers-Briggs type may be, we all need quiet, private, self-nurturing time at least on occasion. We all need time to reflect on what a particular relationship means in order to build and grow (or sometimes repair) the relationship. We all need to silently reflect on our sense of self in order to have or develop an authentic self to share with others. No person can be unceasingly social. We fuel ourselves for relationships by retreating from time to time to a place of reflective solitude.

"Me time" is not merely reflective, of course. It is also restorative. To involve yourself in an activity in which you delight (and which is best done solo) in no way denigrates the nature of your romantic attachment to another person. An acquaintance who is a gifted artist specializing in oil paints said to me, "I cannot address canvas and conversation at the same time." Her painting is something she has to do alone in silence, focusing purely and solely on the picture in her head and its coming to life on canvas. That cannot be done while talking with another person in the room or chit-chatting on her cell phone. By her own confession, her life is empowered by the time she spends painting, and that spills over into other times of her life. There is a richer self to share with her lover and friends and children because she has nurtured that self by observing "me time." For you it may be journaling. Or meditating. Or yoga. Or prayer. Or putting on headphones and listening to Bach, Sarah Brightman, or Beyoncé. Whatever your source of inner renewal may be, "me time" enhances "our time." If you tend to the health of your spirit (your essence), then there will be more of that spirit to share lovingly with those who care and long for you.

7. RELATIONSHIP SHOULD NOT REPLACE ROMANCE.

A healthy couple does not mature from passion to friendship. It should never be either-or. From start to finish, they should be both-and. That is why couples who regularly set aside and diligently protect date nights are making a wise investment in the long-term health of their connection.

Romance is not merely about sexual intimacy or the frequency of such encounters. The Kinsey Institute reports that 36.4 percent of couples in their mid-to-late twenties engage in sexual activity "a few times a month to weekly," whereas only 20.5 percent of couples in their mid-to-late sixties do so. However, well over 70 percent of couples in the sixties-plus age category still claim to be sexually active, though simply with somewhat decreased frequency.[17] It's not the amount but the expression of intimacy that matters, confirming that a couple has not allowed romance to be extinguished over time.

But there is much more to romance than physical expression. It does, in fact, include many of the things that Hollywood and Hallmark suggest. Romance is listening. It is also happily being present for each other without a need for words. It is long walks and hand-holding. It is an occasional

---

[17] www.kinseyinstitute.org/resources/FAQ.html#frequency.

love note left on the dressing table or under the pillow. It is a gift on no special occasion and for no particular reason. It is dancing to the song that takes you back to your very first dance. It is sensitivity and compassion and tenderness and forgiveness and compliments.

As this chapter seeks to point out, creating and sustaining a romantic relationship is not an easy thing to do. It requires hard work and sincere intentionality. As time passes, it is far too easy to unconsciously allow our priorities to be rearranged: to focus on paying the mortgage and doing the shopping and taking care of the kids and attending the meetings and venting the complaints and managing the business. Meanwhile, that which first drew us together and made us desire to create a mutual life journey is neglected. Romance left unattended affects almost everything else in the arena of shared life. Never let the business of maintaining a relationship diminish the romance that gave birth to the relationship in the first place. As noted, it is not either-or. It must always remain both-and.

8. KEEP A BABYSITTER'S PHONE NUMBER CLOSE AT HAND, AND BE SURE TO USE IT!

It is undeniable that one of the greatest gifts in life is family, the birth of a child or children. This milestone also presents one of the greatest challenges to keeping romance alive. An NBC TV comedy of a few years ago called *Up All Night* was built on the very premise that the introduction of a child into a relationship can change and challenge the nature of the relationship on virtually every level.

Loving one's children does not mean investing all of one's love in them only. Love is the one emotional commodity that is limitless in supply. You always have enough for everyone if you are willing to use it. Although children capture the heart in a way no one and nothing else can, romantic love (and the person for whom it is felt) also captures the heart in a genuinely unique way. One should not usurp the other. To allow romance to diminish after parenthood will ultimately do a disservice to your children. It will create before them a model of spousal or partnering relationships that misses a vital link. It will establish for them a set of low and unfulfilling expectations vis-à-vis long-term relationships. And it could eventuate in their having to experience the separation of parents.

So what are some reasonable tips for keeping the romance alive after additional people are introduced to the household?[18] Try the following on as a starter kit list, and then add to it in ways that are pertinent to your own relationship.

ESTABLISH "DATE NIGHT."

This is a common practice among countless couples who are intentional about making the health of the relationship an ongoing priority. Every couple is well advised to set aside some time simply for each other, no one else included. When you were involved in courtship, did you allow members of the extended family to go on your dates with you? That dynamic should not change. "Date Night" injects fun into a relationship again and is a proven antidote to fatigue (whether by that we mean physical fatigue or relational fatigue). No relationship can

---

[18] (Note: Whereas we ordinarily think of the arrival of a child when addressing this topic, it also applies to caregiving for an aging live-in parent or relative or sometimes even the introduction of a pet into the family unit.)

stay healthy without both parties consciously working to maintain its health.

HONOR ADULT CONVERSATION.

The sum of every conversation at the dinner table should not be about homework or that day's experiences at dance or soccer practice. That should be part of the conversation, but the adults in the room should do their own reporting as well. Otherwise, an adult partner may feel his or her daily life is no longer of particular interest to the rest of the family. All family members are of inestimable importance, and to ignore the story of an adult is no more acceptable than to ignore the story of a child.

Honoring adult conversation also (maybe especially) applies to "Date Night." Couples should establish a covenant that they will spend the majority of that evening discussing topics that would bring them together in a dating relationship. If you go to dinner and spend the entire evening discussing what to do about Joey's ADHD or how to afford the prom dress for Melissa, then you may as well have brought Joey and Melissa along. The same is true of pillow talk. Obviously before falling asleep, couples discuss what is uppermost in their minds. But if that topic is always the kids (or finances or schedules, etc.), then a person will eventually realize that he or she is never uppermost in the thoughts of their significant other.

SCHEDULE OCCASIONAL GETAWAYS.

For most of us, "vacation" is family time. We create memories with our children and extended family. Those become cherished treasures to hold on to when our children are grown and have their own children. They are also warm and loving memories for those children when they become adults with their own primary family units. However, a healthy practice for spouses or partners is to occasionally secure childcare in the home and then spend a weekend away as a couple. Romance, intimacy, and simple fun are renewed and restored in settings where couples relate one-on-one without any additional parties participating in the occasion. We simply have to create windows of time just for each other in order to keep a relationship vibrant and vital.

MAKE THE BED A SACRED SPACE, NOT A SHARED SPACE.

Relationship therapists are not of one mind about this, but most tend to agree that there needs to be some space that is reserved just for the couple. That is symbolic of the fact that there is a unique "us," and that at least one place in the world exists where two people simply belong to each other. This is not to say that children should never be allowed in the parents' bedroom or be barred from the bed itself. But when sleep time comes, children should be in their own beds. Once children are past about six months old, it is reasonable that their own beds exist in their own rooms. And for those who care about intimacy, from sex to snuggling, pets should not spend the night on the bed, either.

FIDELITY MATTERS.

We know, of course, that couples can and do survive acts of infidelity. But we also know that just as many couples do not survive them. Ruth Houston, founder of infidelity. com and author of *Is He Cheating On You?*, estimates that approximately half of all marriages affected by adultery do not survive.[19] And even if you do the hard work to get through that experience, the pain factor for everyone involved is undeniable. Restoring trust can take a long time and a great deal of labor to accomplish. A sense of self and self-worth is demeaned. A sense of respect for the partner who was unfaithful is diminished. Physical intimacy, while not always compromised by the experience, can begin to prompt feelings of sadness: "This is no longer our unique expression of love," "I must not be sufficient as a lover," or "It is merely biological as opposed to emotional." Once a couple has committed to a monogamous relationship, both partners should do all within their power to honor that commitment. And should intimacy issues emerge, they should be honestly addressed with each other. If needed, those conversations can occur in the presence of a trained listener. Fidelity matters, and no temporarily popular trends (such as "free love" or "open marriage") have ever ultimately altered that.

The bottom line is that every couple must be diligent in protecting the essential quality of "us." And whereas numerous other people have vital roles in our lives, there must be some points and places where two partners establish sacred space and time simply for each other with those boundaries not transgressed by anyone else.

9. REMEMBER THAT BEING IN LOVE IS FUN!

If that were not so, who would want to be in love in the first place? Why would anyone write love songs and sonnets if loving were a chore? Being in a healthy relationship with

---

[19]   Ruth Houston, *Is He Cheating On You?* (Corona, NY: Lifestyle Publications, 2002).

a significant other is one of life's most authentic delights. How many people have you known who, following the death of a beloved spouse, are quick to say, "I want to be married again"? The experience of loving and being loved brings a type of bliss that is truly not replicated in any other loving relationship. Being in love is fun.

A notice appeared in the Classified Ads section of a small-town newspaper. Apparently the person typing the ad didn't spell-check before printing. It was intended to read, "Perfect starter apartment for newlywed couple. Affordably priced. Comes furnished." The typist, however, inadvertently omitted the "r" from the word "furnished." Thus, the word appeared in the ad as "funished." Personally, I prefer the accidental word that resulted. Love authentically expressed and experienced is likewise authentically fun. Note again the significance of a single letter in a word; change the "u" to an "i" and "funished" becomes "finished." A sure way to quickly finish a romance is take the fun out of it. So, whatever you do as a couple that brings mutual enjoyment, laughter, celebration, and special closeness, keep doing it. And do it often. Make certain that your relationship comes "funished."

10. DO NOT LET OTHERS DEFINE ROMANCE FOR YOU.

This is the capstone piece of advice for any couple. Do not let a movie define it. Do not let a romance novel define it. Do not let Viagra commercials define it. Do not let your buddies or friends at the office define it. Romance is what it is for you, and that is all that matters. For some, it is dinner and dancing; for others, it is sitting at a campsite, charcoaling the fish you just caught together in a nearby stream. Only you can decide what "romance" means in your relationship.

In most traditional wedding ceremonies, there are vows with which each partner promises the other "to love and to cherish for better or worse, for richer or poorer, in sickness and in health, till death do us part." The beauty and richness of that vow is that it promises each partner they will have someone with whom to journey for the long haul. It transcends the shallowness and sadness of the occasional celebrity marriage we read about that lasts two or three months. At its heart, romance is covenant. It is the assurance that someone plans to walk through life with us, "for better or worse, in sickness and in health, till death do us part."

~~~

Joe and Sarah were about to celebrate their fiftieth wedding anniversary. A quiet couple, their plans were simply to have dinner together at their favorite restaurant and then return home. But their children had other ideas. Fifty years is a singularly important occasion, and so (against their parents' protests) the children decided to have an anniversary banquet in a large hall at a local club. Relatives and friends from all across the country were invited to come to the party in the couple's hometown of Seattle.

When the date arrived, almost one hundred people gathered to offer love, thanks, and best wishes to Sarah and Joe. Following dinner came a time for toasts. A nephew from the East Coast hoisted a glass of champagne and, attempting to be respectfully humorous, said,

"Wow! Fifty years with the same person … that's a really long time!"

Everyone chuckled. When the laughter subsided, Joe looked at his wife, smiled lovingly, and said, "Yes. Fifty years is a long time. But it would have been a lot longer without her."

Joe and Sarah had found the beauty of having someone to count on for the journey. And in so doing, they discovered substantive romance. The nephew's joking remark underscored a commonly-held suspicion that variety may well be the spice of life. But Joe's response indicated a different belief. For Sarah and him, trust, companionship, shared values, and facing whatever is out there together, for better or worse, constituted the foundation of romance as they understood it.

~~~

Do not let others define "romance" for you. It varies couple by couple. Obviously there are certain suggestions you can heed that will deepen and enhance it. That's what this chapter has sought to address. But ultimately only you and your spouse or partner know what keeps the fires alive in your relationship. Identify those principles. Live by them. Honor them. Protect them. The return is more than worth whatever investment you make.

LOVE AS COMMUNITY

*T*here really is no such thing as love in isolation. We are created to be social entities. We are designed for relationships.

To be sure, there are hermits who love nature and, to the extent possible, avoid human contact. There are recluses who love to be with self more than with others. There are ascetics who love God but do so in almost complete solitude. There are people who lock themselves away from neighbors but live with houses full of pets. But life in the real world ordinarily dictates that we develop a sense of community. By that I simply mean that we must create a way of relating to and dealing with others. Why? Because others are undeniable realities in our world. And how we choose to treat and interact with them absolutely determines how we ourselves will be treated. The quality of our lives, to a great extent, depends upon our relational philosophy.

In order to successfully live "in community" and thus to enhance the general quality of life therein (including, obviously, the quality of our own lives), a handful of givens need to be stated and carefully considered. Let's think about them together.

1. PRACTICE THE FINE ART OF LISTENING.

There's an adage that says: "God gave us two ears and only one mouth. Pay attention!" Though humorous in intent, those are also words of wisdom worth considering. Few things make others feel more valued than simply being heard. That does not always mean agreeing with their opinions, but it does mean lending an attentive ear to them.

One of the most successful politicians I know is a master in the town hall meeting. When he arrives for a gathering of his constituents, he always brings an assistant with him, whom he seats prominently at the front of the room. He sets aside no more than ten minutes to speak to whatever issue is pertinent in that place at that moment, and then he says, "I've talked enough. My purpose tonight is to listen while you talk." Then, pointing to his assistant seated at the front, he continues, "This is _____. Speak clearly, as she is going to take down what you say. When I get back to Washington, I want to read over your remarks because I take your ideas seriously." Whether or not he reads the notes is anyone's guess. I have no reason to think he is less than honest when he makes that promise, but the point is that his constituents think what they say matters to him. He makes them feel heard and honored. And in turn, they keep re-electing him, whatever the current political tides happen to be.

We all have had moments when we were speaking to someone else whose eyes glazed over ... or who kept glancing at her watch ... or who continued to interrupt, anxious to tell his story and turn us into his listeners ... or who would peer over our shoulders to see if a more attractive conversation partner was in the room. By the same token, all of us have been in conversations with individuals whose attentiveness made us say, "She listened to me as if I were her very dearest friend." Instinctively, we are drawn to people who make us feel valued with their listening skills, as if what we have to say truly matters. If we're drawn to others who make us feel that way, then obviously others will be drawn to us for doing likewise.

2. SEEK TO IDENTIFY AND EMPATHIZE WITH OTHER PEOPLE.

A stock response in corporate conversations is "I hear what you're saying." But that alone is not always enough. Often we want to respond, "But can you feel what I'm feeling?"

An important attribute of love is compassion. In some cultures, the word "compassion" literally means "to see with the eyes of the other." What an incredibly important (and community-building) attribute! One of my children, a professional therapist, often remarks that what a client says is not as important as why the client said it. Can we get to the feeling level beneath the words, to the emotions that drive the statements, to the person behind the voice? Individuals feel loved not simply when they feel "heard" but when they feel "known" (understood and acknowledged). Thus, life in community is enhanced when we seek "to see with the eyes of the other," to discern why people speak, decide, and behave as they do.

Apply this principle to whatever arena of community you choose. It is almost universally pertinent. A simple illustration could be in the area of politics. Suppose (a huge word in this particular context) that elected officials in Washington would seek to honestly and accurately hear another person's or party's statements? Could the gridlock that most of us decry and deplore be resolved if, in fact, those who represent us would simply listen to one another with our best interests at heart? What if elected officials, prior to pontificating from the motivations of remaining partisan or appealing to voters, would actually listen to the other side during key debates? Is it possible that said elected officials could learn something via focused listening, perhaps even that the two sides were not always as polemically separated as initially imagined, or that there is almost always a way to arrive at respectful (and politically productive) compromise? Suppose Democrats and Republicans approached budgetary issues no longer so determined to emerge "victorious" as to remain faithful to their constituents and their conscience, and thus they actually listened to and seriously considered what those on the other side of the aisle were saying and why they said it? And (assuming that miracles still sometimes happen), what if those politicians, before subjecting their nation to vitriolic debates and accusations (and thus decreasing public confidence and personal dignity), asked the question, "What is the loving course of action at this point? Having heard the other side and having considered what they had to say, whether or not I fully agree, how can I proceed in such fashion as to love my country and bring healing and strength?" Authentic (empathic) listening is a healthy course of action that enhances virtually any interpersonal or community relationship.

3. DO NOT FORGET THE ALMOST UNPARALLELED IMPORTANCE OF COMMUNICATION IN FOSTERING FRIENDSHIPS AND EXPRESSING LOVE.

This is the logical extension of the first two suggestions. It is nothing more than simple deductive reasoning: if we listen appropriately, and if we identify with the feelings of the one to whom we listened, then we are establishing a relationship of honest and healthy communication.

As previously noted, marital therapists used to suggest that marriages rise or fall based on at least one of four factors: (a) finances, (b) extended family, (c) sex, or (d) conflicting career demands. Now, most therapists seem to agree that the key to healthy relationships is communication skills. When those skills are present, then, should problems arise in any of the other areas, the partners will have the requisite abilities to discuss, assess, address, and process the issues at hand. If, however, the couple lacks the ability (or willingness) to become involved in serious communications, then the problem at hand is exacerbated and can spell the end of the relationship. Afterward, either party may claim, "He couldn't break free from his mother's apron strings," "She consistently spent more money than we earned," or any number of other projected reasons for the end of the relationship. However, the real culprit was an inability (or lack of willingness) to honestly discuss and resolve the issue at hand.

When issues are sufficiently serious, I always suggest that individuals seek the assistance of a trained listener (a counselor, spiritual leader, or therapist). However, the communication process is certainly enhanced even without a trained listener, if competent psychotherapeutic methods are employed. This is true not just for couples, but for the variety of relationships found within a community. Any relationship experiencing crisis has a far greater chance of positive resolution if the participants use a Rogerian approach[20] in communicating. That method begins with one person saying to the other, "I hear you saying that _____. Am I correct? Is that what you are actually saying?" This simple act indicates a sincere desire to fully understand the other (in and of itself, an expression of compassion) and greatly increases the possibility of crisis resolution. That being said, it is still undeniably true that certain situations are best addressed by engaging a trained listener as a third party in the process of communication.

4. CHOOSE YOUR BATTLES.

Not every issue is worthy of the stress that results from interpersonal conflict. Just face it. Most of the things we argue about are not worth the time, the energy, or the potentially negative ramifications involved. "Why do you insist on squeezing the toothpaste tube from the middle?" "Why can you never put the aspirin bottle back in the medicine cabinet?" "Why do you always salt your food before tasting it?" "Why do you change the settings on the radio in my car?" Before launching into a conflict based on

[20] Carl Rogers (1902–1987) was the father of "client-centered therapy" and was nominated for the Nobel Peace Prize for his use of an empathic approach of counseling to help ameliorate political tensions in South Africa and Northern Ireland.

any of those questions or a thousand others like them, first ask yourself, "Why does it matter?" At what point are you willing to allow something trivial to interrupt or damage something crucial?

～～

A friend told me of a young engaged couple who had been deeply in love but whose relationship ended. He was not abusive. She was not unfaithful. He was affirming and charming. She was loving and attentive. They seemed compatible in all the ways that are positive indicators for successful relationships. His parents were, therefore, understandably surprised when the young man came home one evening and announced that he had broken off the romance. The young man, a University of Michigan graduate and avid football fan, explained, "I just cannot spend the rest of my life with a woman who went to Ohio State!" Were it not a true story, it would be comical. But the truth is that he allowed loyalty to a football team to supersede human love, and there is nothing funny (or logical) about that.

～～

To live positively and lovingly within a community, you must know how to choose your battles. Sometimes those moments are obvious. A rather famous woman publicly chronicled her lifelong battle with addiction. She described how her father, himself an addict, introduced her to narcotics when she was still a preteen. As children naturally do, she craved her father's attention and love. So she willingly joined him in his ritual of getting high. He became a playmate, apparently not possessing the requisite emotional maturity to function as a parent. His daughter became not so much his child as his buddy. The relationship was mutually satisfying, but in an improper and patently unhealthy way. Ultimately, she sacrificed a great deal in terms of friends, academics, physical health, and self-respect, jeopardizing her life in the process. At some point, someone should have intervened. Surely, given the social nature of the setting as she described it, and the scores of people passing in and out of their home, there had to be some indication, some hint that the father–child relationship had gone awry. The loving path to take at that point would've been to say, "No! These are lines that cannot be crossed." The father's life would have been remarkably altered, no doubt. And it's likely that the child would've responded with significant anger, trying (again naturally) to defend her parent. And yet, to act lovingly would have required intervention, whatever the cost. There are times when silence is not golden, but instead can be damaging to the point of being deadly. Some battles have to be fought.

Is the other person dishonest? Immoral? Involved in something illegal? Abusive? Insanely jealous? Does he steal your money? Does she hate your family and friends? Does he intentionally say or do things to damage your ego in an attempt to manipulate and control you? Does she frequently negatively contrast you to other people? Is there sexual incompatibility? Neglect? A blatant disregard for your values? Is he or she, as your employer or supervisor, demanding you to do things that are clearly unethical? If you're going to draw a line in the sand, make it a line worth drawing. Fight about things that have significant worth. Or, if the issue is serious enough, forget fighting and simply walk away. But choose your battles wisely. It is simply foolish to squander the opportunity for love and the joy that accompanies it because the other person squeezes the toothpaste tube from the middle or cheers for the wrong sports team!

5. CHOOSE HOW YOU WILL CONDUCT YOUR BATTLES.

Whereas the majority of issues that result in conflict are probably not worth the energy or the aftermath, there are undeniable lines that must be drawn in the sand. As noted, abusiveness, dishonesty, infidelity, actions that demean or damage ego strengths, manipulation, pressure to do that which we consider unethical, activities that threaten the well-being of others, and certain other sources of anxiety or pain cannot afford to be dismissed or denied.

Sooner or later, all of us who live in community with others will experience moments when our level of discomfort sets off a warning siren that needs to be heard and honored. When those moments come, resolving them as lovingly as possible is the goal. Again, proper attention to empathic communications is key.

～

One of the most intellectually-gifted men I know has a history of moving from job to job with Indy 500 speed. Because of the undeniable presence of his keen ability, employers keep taking chances on him. He is articulate and can be charming in an interview setting. However, one of the realities of life is conflict, especially within the marketplace. And that is a reality this gentleman has never learned to navigate. His response to the slightest annoyance, and sometimes merely to normal acts of supervision, is to become livid and adversarial. He erupts at coworkers who dare to make suggestions regarding his job, even to those who have been assigned a partnering role with him. He accuses and demeans. Because of his considerable intellectual skills, he is quite the opponent when it comes to debate. However, most of the time his coworkers or supervisors have no intention of being "opponents." He sees any disagreement, however minimal, as a direct challenge not merely to his job performance but to his very being. And so he responds by verbally assaulting the person who has caused his momentary discomfort. The result is that this truly talented man has never stayed at a job for a significant stretch of time. His anger mismanagement has made certain of that.

What if that man had made the decision long ago to practice the positive craft of active loving? What if prior to his outbursts or tirades, he were to pause and ask himself, "What is the loving response to make in this situation?" How many job-ending conflicts could thus have been easily resolved with virtually no negative consequences whatsoever?

Or what if he had learned to practice empathic listening in conversations on the job? "Let me make sure I understand what you're saying. I heard you say _____. Is that what you intended?" Many times what someone means to say and what we hear are two very different things, and conflict can be resolved (or, better yet, avoided) by simple clarification.

Or what if he had made a deliberate decision to respond with non-adversarial honesty, as opposed to anger? A helpful course of action might be to delay any immediate reply to a remark that is discomforting. Let some time pass. Then, approach the other person calmly and simply be forthright: "I value our relationship, and I don't want to see anything jeopardize it. So out of respect for that and for you, I need to tell you that what you said/did earlier today troubled me. I have thought about it and tried to process it, but I want to be fair with you. Maybe you didn't intend to communicate what I felt from you. So, can we talk about what happened? I want to hear from you what you really meant, and I want you to know how I really felt. And, most of all, I want us to move forward as friends." Such an approach in no way avoids the issue at hand but instead addresses it in a fashion that offers the possibility for healing and an ongoing relationship. If my acquaintance had simply learned alternative (and not particularly difficult) approaches to conflict resolution, his résumé would likely not be littered with so many short-stay employments.

～～～

Life in community assures us that there will be moments of conflict. That is a given. However, how we conduct our battles usually determines whether the conflicts will be debilitating or mere bumps in the road. Even in moments of conflict, as we choose how to respond, the question that brings long-term peace is simply, "What is the honest and loving thing to do?"

6. HONOR THE VALUE OF MULLIGANS.

Previously alluded to, a "mulligan" is a golfing term that refers to being given a second chance to drive the ball down the fairway (when the first drive was erratic). The first shot off the tee on any hole in the game of golf is called "the drive." For Rory McIlroy or Michelle Wie, mulligans are moot points. Those pros drive the ball long and straight. Furthermore, professional golf does not allow mulligans. However, for those of us who have no idea where the ball is going when we strike it, there is often the understanding that on one hole per every nine we can use a mulligan. It is literally a "do-over." In life, "do-over's" are not only acceptable but often imperative if love is to flourish. And given the fact that it is impossible to rewrite history (and that "forgive and forget" is equally impossible, as those who forgive still retain a sense of memory), then where "do-over's" cannot be established, at least "start-over's" can.

Take divorce as an example. It is unquestionably a tragic conclusion to what started out as a dream of happiness and wholeness. Even so, in American society almost half of married couples see that dream die via divorce. Many others permanently separate without signing the final documents dissolving the marriage (though, in essence, the marriage has ended). Although one reads the occasional account of a divorced couple deciding to re-wed, in the vast majority of divorces, "over" means "over." However, though it is rare that a divorced couple opts for a "do-over," the majority do at some point embark on a "start-over."

If one is wise, he or she reflects on what occurred in the previous prematurely-concluded relationship so as to learn how to make the next one last. One might ask:

- What priorities did I allow to interfere with my marriage?

- Could I have been more effective in the allotment of my time?

- Did I mishandle issues with extended family that negatively impacted my primary relationship?

- Were there moments when I could have arrived at an acceptable place of compromise, but adopted and maintained an intractable position?

- Did I fail to express love verbally or visibly?

There are occasions in life when the possibility of a mulligan no longer exists, but the possibility of a fresh start in a new relationship does. And the fresh start can be enhanced and enriched if we learn lessons from previous experiences, even those that involved painful conclusions. Put another way, we can live the life of loving by remembering and learning from prior experiences when we did not make love our first priority.

Likewise, not every experience that is negatively concluded is forever ended. Again, we can use divorce as an illustration. Former spouses usually retain some ongoing points of connection. The most obvious that springs to mind is children. Whereas many spouses do not remain husband and wife, they do forever remain mom and dad. Thus, they inevitably relate. Though the marriage may not have lasted, there is no reason why their future moments of relation should not be loving. That is true for numerous reasons, not the least of which is each parent's devotion to the children. Witnessing ongoing hostility between parents provides no long-term benefits to children. As noted, forgetting may not be possible, but forgiving and moving forward are. Furthermore, children aside, bearing resentment against a former partner is a kind of self-inflicted emotional pain that you simply should not choose to endure. The old adage makes good sense: "Move out, and move on." The baggage of anger or resentment stands in the way of healthily and happily moving on with life. Though romantic love may not have been permanently achieved, that does not preclude the possibility of two former partners dealing with one another lovingly and respectfully. Ultimately, to offer that love to the other (whether or not we are convinced they deserve it) affords peace and release to us, thus making it possible to realize the beauty of fresh starts.

The Mulligan Principle applies in countless ways as we live in community. Whether in romantic, business, or political relations, or in dealings with neighbors, relatives, or friends, we cannot change that which is past. But we can learn from it in order to build a happier future. To reflect on the moments when we did not live lovingly educates us for more productive love and life yet to come.

7. GIVE BACK BY PAYING FORWARD.

This is an individual commitment to creating a strong and loving sense of community.

Those who serve as sponsors with Alcoholics Anonymous give back by paying forward. At some point in time, someone assisted them on their journey toward sobriety. Without that person's assistance, they may well have fallen into permanent relapse. But through the gentle, non-judgmental presence of their sponsor (comforting, counseling, listening, and encouraging), they made the long voyage to a new, healthy, holistic way of living. Sometimes the voyage involved taking two steps forward and one step back, but the sponsor was always present to help turn the person making the pilgrimage in the right direction again. Once sobriety has been attained and maintained, the person who received help desires to give help. Someone else is walking where he or she previously walked. Someone else needs similar assistance, presence, nurture, and understanding. So the care-receiver–turned–caregiver repays the favor by offering the same favor to someone else. That's what is meant by the phrase "paying it forward." And, when one after another after yet another does so, a larger community comes into being. It is the community of recovery—a place where people belong, are supported, affirmed, or helped when needed, and then are afforded the opportunity to help others. It becomes, in the best sense of the phrase, a community of love.

Some teachers are committed to students because special teachers were once committed to them. Some clergy and therapists help those struggling because they themselves were once helped. Some coaches seek to develop character as much as skill in young athletes because other coaches instilled morals and values in them. Some laborers make extra efforts to produce quality products because someone convinced them of the inestimable beauty of doing one's best. Some politicians place patriotism above partisanship because they were inspired by a previous statesman who dared to do the same. All those people and thousands of others like them enhance our sense of community by "paying it forward," by giving back to the world what was previously given to them.

✧

A woman I knew years ago spent most of her adult life actively involved with the Girl Scouts program. Though she never married and became a mom, she would proudly tell anyone within earshot, "I have been mama to over five

117

hundred girls across the years." Her influence on the lives of young women was beyond description, as attested to by the love they showered upon her, the scouting awards that came her way, and the outpouring of thanks and affection from successful woman after successful woman who spoke at her memorial service.

She had grown up in a home of abject poverty. Her parents were constantly exhausted by trying to keep a roof over the heads of and food on the table for four young children in an economically-depressed mining village. However, every Tuesday afternoon she walked two miles to a small Lutheran church where the Girl Scouts met. She described it as "the one breath of fresh air in my dusty world." There, adult counselors knew her, nurtured her, and inspired her to broaden her horizons, to think of education and career and a new life in a different world. "All that I am," she told me, "is because of those kind women who paid for my uniform and bought my badges and complimented my work and taught me to dream dreams that were bigger than I had dreamt before." Her profound and pronounced influence that carried on in the lives of others, her very life's legacy, all resulted from a sense of gratitude and a desire to pay the debt forward.

8. INVEST IN COMMUNITY.

By this I mean that we are all well advised to be part of a corporate commitment to creating a strong and loving environment.

Some words of wisdom are, "No one can do everything, but everyone can do something." And often the something I can do is simply to ally myself with an organization of others who can do many things. It is the cumulative effect of individual people bound together that transforms communities.

Neither Susan B. Anthony nor Carrie Chapman Catt nor Alice Paul could have turned the tide in the women's suffrage movement by marching solo. But, because they gathered a sea of like-minded women (and men) to stand with them, in 1918 Congress passed what was two years later to become the Nineteenth Amendment (upon ratification by a sufficient number of states). For all his brilliance and prowess, Martin Luther King, Jr., would not have accomplished what he did had he made his freedom marches alone. It took a community of similarly committed individuals marching alongside him to usher in a new day of desegregation and the long-overdue movement toward racial equality. A church is more than a single minister, a mosque is more than an imam, and a synagogue more than a rabbi, however talented those individuals may be. There is power inherent in community.

So to make a loving difference in the world, usually we must connect with organizations or institutions that put love into practice. Recently my wife and I joined a number of friends to attend the annual Habitat for Humanity Awards Banquet in New York City. Several hundred people gathered to view videos and hear testimonies from people whose lives have been changed by that wonderful organization founded by the late Millard Fuller. One award recipient was a man who has donated multiple millions of dollars to Habitat's efforts. Another was a single mother of four whose family now lives in decent housing because of Habitat and who regularly assists in the building of new homes for others. She "pays it forward," but does so as part of a larger team.

One person is able to give millions. Another is able to give time and sweat equity. And interestingly, each of them said the same thing in their acceptance speech, almost using the very same words. Each said they were "privileged" to join hands and hearts with a large family of human helpers, doing together what no one person could ever accomplish alone. That is the beauty of finding a helping institution. Every city and town has a cadre of such agencies that need volunteers. No one person can do all things, but a body of like-minded people working together can make miracles happen. Love is often the result of community, people bonded together by a gallant and shared desire to make the world a better and brighter place.

9. DO A PERIODIC PERSONALITY ASSESSMENT.

An important question to ponder from time to time is, "Do I make loving easy or challenging?" Most of the time, the Golden Rule is a good rule to follow, which is doubtless why a version of it appears in the texts of twenty-one world religions including Judaism, Christianity, Islam, Hinduism, Confucianism, Buddhism, Taoism, and Zoroastrianism, as well as in the works of countless humanistic ethicists. People tend to treat us similarly to the ways we treat them.

Unless I choose to live alone on a desert island, I cannot avoid or ignore my relatedness to other people. Community is a given. How I function within it is a choice that I make. My way of relating to others plays a role in whether or not love is ultimately able to flourish in the world, or, at least, in my little corner of it.

Let's say you arrive at your job as an office manager and receive from your CEO an anxiety-producing e-mail asking why your production numbers are not increasing. Your fear and frustration spill out in your next encounter with a subordinate who feels abused by the harshness of your words but not sufficiently empowered to honestly respond to them. He, in turn, is impatient with his administrative assistant, who criticizes the FedEx deliveryman for being late, who harasses the waitress for getting his lunch order wrong, who yells at the taxi driver for taking a slower route, who goes home and lashes out at his child for not having all his homework done, who storms out of the room and kicks the dog! And anywhere along the line, any of those people could have broken the chain. Did each have a right to feel unfairly treated or personally frustrated? Of course they did. But, did each also have the authority to make a personal choice about how to treat others? Again, of course they did! At some point we simply choose love, whether or not we've been treated lovingly. We choose to create a ripple that has the potential to infuse the community with a different power than that with which we were touched.

A periodic personality assessment is merely a matter of saying to oneself, "What am I passing along to those around me? For they may well pass it on to others, and they to others, until it reaches me again. Do I choose patience, forgiveness, kindness, courtesy, and smiles? Because every loving choice I make plants seeds that grow in the culture of my community. Do I want a different world than the one in which I am living? If so, then creating that new world begins with me."

SEVEN

MOVING FORWARD FROM LOST LOVE

Years ago a popular singer, the late Laura Branigan, scored big with a plaintive ballad in which she asked, "How am I supposed to live without you?"[21] There are answers to that question, and we will take a look at them in this chapter. But if we tweak Ms. Branigan's plea minimally and ask instead, "Can I live without you?" the answer is clearly "Yes." Moving forward after a lost love is not easy, but it is entirely possible. In fact, what other reasonable choice do people have? Moving forward to the place psychologists call "new normal" is not a matter of "if," it is simply a matter of "how."

The simple truth is that sooner or later all good things do, in fact, come to an end.

---

21 Michael Bolton and Doug James, "How Am I Supposed to Live Without You?" *Branigan 2*, Atlantic Records, 1983.

- Every romantic relationship will eventually conclude, whether through separation, divorce, or death.

- We eventually lose grandparents and parents, friends, and siblings.

- We lose boyfriends and girlfriends who love us for a season but whose love for us turns out not to be as strong as ours for them.

- We lose jobs and homes.

- We lose heroes.

- We lose pets.

- We sometimes lose self-confidence or self-esteem.

- With age or illness, we lose the ability to do certain things we used to do well or, at least, things we enjoyed doing.

Loss is an undeniable reality of life. Sometimes it is part of the developmental process and gives way to another life epoch that is longed for and celebrated. Even so, letting go of the previous epoch and its inherent joys is a form of loss. I remember when our daughter, Alison, was planning her wedding to a fine young man who is loving and ethical, caring and gentle. She and he were educated at the same college, were in their mid-twenties, had known each other for several years, and were deeply in love. Everything about the relationship and the upcoming marriage seemed right. And yet, all the gladness surrounding the big event did not eradicate a certain kind of sadness at the loss of what had been. Prior to the wedding, she and her mother went on a trip to Europe. Upon returning, my wife said to me, "This is the last time Alison and I will travel as mother and little girl. In the future, my baby will be someone's wife." And that someone, though genuinely loved by the entire family, took on certain roles that we had to release.

A friend at last received the promotion he had long awaited in his corporation. He had worked and yearned for the move for almost twenty years. Finally, it was his. He embraced it with joy and passion. And yet, he also confessed that he wept when saying goodbye to his current staff. They were "his team," many of them almost like family. He also wept when driving away from the house in the town where so many wonderful memories had been made with his family over the course of two decades. Even in the experience of gain that had been anticipated and desired for years, there was still an experience of loss.

Live long enough and you will lose something or someone you love. Live longer, and you will lose more. So how do we cope with that? How do we learn to effectively let go and move forward? We can start by remembering these things:

1. LOSS DOES NOT PRECLUDE GAIN.

Tennyson was correct when he wrote with a broken heart, following the death of his best friend (and his sister's fiancé):

> I hold it true, whate'er befall,
> I feel it when I sorrow most,
> 'Tis better to have loved and lost
> Than never to have loved at all.[22]

---

[22] Alfred Lord Tennyson, "In Memoriam A.H.H.," *Masterpieces of Religious Verse,* James Dalton Morrison (ed.) (New York: Harper and Brothers, 1949), p. 298.

Ask managers of major league baseball teams who were eventually replaced by the front office if they regret having managed. Ask widows or widowers who had long and happy marriages if the grief they experienced would cause them, if they had it to do over again, to remain single. The joy of loving is in no way eradicated by the loss of love. Whereas experience certainly differs from memory, memory can be a wonderful thing. Likewise, the lessons learned from previous loves live on, enabling and empowering us in the future, even if those particular loves can never return. Loss in life is inevitable. However, loss does not preclude gain. It does not remove from the shelves of our lives that which the love, however brief, awarded us.

2. THE LOSS OF LOVE IS A LEARNING EXPERIENCE.

As a respected writer reminds us, "The effects on a relationship when both people do inquiry can be nothing short of miraculous."[23]

To engage in reflection following the loss of love teaches me what I value in a person, thing, or experience. Two young women with whom I have worked in the past illustrate this principle for me. One was divorced. The other ended a long-term relationship with a partner when she learned the man she loved had been unfaithful.

The woman who went through the divorce confessed that she desired marriage and family, but she needed someone who was likewise invested in those disciplines. Her former husband had been married to his work. Though never unfaithful in the traditional understanding of the term, he did not allocate sufficient time to be with her and

---

[23] Byron Katie, op. cit., 195.

their children, nor did he give evidence of being particularly interested in the children's educational or athletic activities. "I want someone who finds as much joy in family as I do," she said. The loss of her first marriage educated her regarding what she deemed as non-negotiable should she ever marry again. Subsequently, she met and fell in love with a man who had a similar commitment to home and family. After many years together, their relationship is intact and a source of deep mutual joy. She learned from lost love and used that insight to construct a stronger love for the future.

Likewise, the other young woman determined quickly that for her, an indispensable component of a romantic relationship had to be trust. No matter how much fun a couple may experience together, no matter how similar their likes and interests, no matter how much passion might be present, and no matter how well they get along with each other's families, a person cannot subject herself to fears and worries whenever her partner is away for any length of time. This young woman learned from a lost love in order to construct a stronger understanding of what love should look like in her future.

A man sat in my study and discussed plans for his upcoming wedding. His first wife had died almost one year earlier. They had been married for twenty-five years. Whereas all marriages have ups and downs, theirs had been a fundamentally happy wedlock. His bride-to-be was nothing like his former wife. Her appearance, her interests, her profession, and more made for an obvious divergence from his first spouse. In the course of our conversation, he made the statement, "I don't need to marry my first wife again, nor is it fair to try to make someone else over in her image. But I do want to come home to love and laughter, as I did in the past." By reflecting on a lost love, he was able to identify the qualities that would make life livable for him in the future.

~~~

Obviously, through careful reflection we learn what to look for and what to avoid in the next experience or relationship. There is wisdom in the idea of, "Once burned, twice shy." However, the loss of love also frequently teaches us how to more effectively assess self, including personal needs, and thus become better at loving others (and, hopefully, at taking specific steps to make love last).

Does the workaholic who ultimately loses his family look inward and learn from the loss? Is he able to say, "My priorities contributed to the death of that relationship, so in a future relationship I will establish a healthier set of priorities"? Does the unfaithful partner look inward and say, "My unwillingness to face relational issues in a constructive way and my sense of entitlement or self-indulgence undid a positive partnership, so I will refrain from entering into a new partnership until I am able to make and honor a monogamous covenant"? Does the man who received a long-awaited promotion that forces his family to change homes look inward and say, "I will determine the tangibles and intangibles that made life so rich and rewarding in my former setting so that we can build a new life in a new setting that is equally satisfying for our family"? If interpreted with wisdom, experiences of pain from the past can provide unparalleled lessons for discovering meaning and satisfaction in the future.

3. NOT EVERYTHING OR EVERYONE I LOVE IS GOOD FOR ME.

I love is good for me. Endings, whether happy or hurtful, remind us of this. For our own well-being, there are times when it is imperative that we let go of things that we may, in fact, actually love.

Many people love tobacco products. But every competent health professional will counsel that such love is detrimental to physical health and, in fact, to survival. Over four hundred and eighty thousand people in the United States alone (and over six million globally) die annually because they choose not to let go of those products.[24]

The same is true regarding the use of recreational drugs, which end countless lives and negatively impact millions of others every year.

In the midst of a national obesity epidemic and subsequent increases in diabetes and heart disease, certainly the foods many of us grew up with and learned to love must be reduced in intake, if not omitted altogether.

Similar to how our love for these things can cause lasting damage, so can the physical and emotional high that some experience via promiscuity or relational infidelity. The results of those activities can result in contracting an STD, destroying a relationship, tarnishing one's reputation, sacrificing a sense of self-esteem, or all of the above. The painful costs of continuing said behavior are too high to justify the momentary pleasures associated with it.

---

[24] National Center for Disease Control, *Health Statistics, United States, 2017.*

A love of power or authority over others or an inordinate love of self drives other people away from us. Thus, those are loves that should be dismissed for our own well-being. An incredibly wealthy oil tycoon of a long-ago generation made the statement from his deathbed that the pain of dying is made worse by the pain of loneliness.

Sometimes divorce (or the dissolution of a primary relationship), though always having an inherently tragic aspect, is the only way to save one's emotional health and occasionally even to save one's physical life. In these cases, walking away is not a sign of failure so much as an indication of wisdom.

4. LOVE LIFE.

A longtime acquaintance has a self-styled license plate on his car. It is the same one that has been displayed on his bumper over many years. It simply reads, "Live Life!" He is determined to enjoy life while he has it, as well as to encourage others to do the same. Whatever losses he may have suffered, he is aware that there are other gains, gifts, and blessings to experience and celebrate. And sometimes the experience of having lost something or someone we love makes us more keenly aware and appreciative of the new experiences or individuals that bring love to our lives.

Years ago, the late Dr. Elisabeth Kübler-Ross wrote a wonderful book built around the theme of loving life while one has it. As both a physician and a therapist, her field of expertise was death and dying. She dealt almost exclusively with terminally ill patients. From that vantage point, she wrote what many consider to be one of her finest works. It was based on her relationships with certain patients who chose to drink each drop from life's cup while they could. She used many of them as the case studies in her book, indicating medically that those who embraced life (even in the face of the certainty of death) survived much longer and had a higher quality of living than others who gave up and gave in. The title of her book is *To Live Until We Say Goodbye*.[25] Even if "goodbye" is far into your future and you have decades yet to live, her title is a helpful mantra for everyone. Just because we have said certain goodbyes is no reason to check out on life before our final goodbye must be said.

Life rushes by. Why would we choose to miss that which is by imprisoning ourselves in grief for that which was? In truth, to do so dishonors the person whom we grieve. Losing a lover—whether to death, separation, divorce, or a breakup—and saying, "I will never love again" calls into question the nature of the preceding relationship. If loving brought joy, then it is purely logical that one would want to discover new love. To intentionally avoid doing so might indicate there was something in the preceding relationship that one does not want to be subjected to again. On the occasion of her second marriage, my friend spoke to me of her first husband, Joe, who had passed on, saying, "Joe loved me too much to want me to be lonely. And I loved him too much to want to live without love."

～～

A man I knew in my hometown spent his professional years as a floral designer. He was able to craft arrangements of indescribable beauty out of blooms, twigs, and blossoms that most of us tend to pass by without noticing. He

---

[25] Elisabeth Kübler-Ross, *To Live Until We Say Goodbye* (New York: Simon and Schuster/Touchstone, 1978).

often confessed, "As much as I love how the flowers look, I love even more how my customers look when they see the flowers." Not long after retiring, he discovered that he missed those customers. He missed being around people on a daily basis. So, somewhat to the surprise of those who knew him, he took a job as a greeter at a local Walmart. A friend asked about his rather dramatic shift in careers. He replied, "It's not that dramatic, really. My greatest joy was bringing joy to my customers. They would begin to smile as soon as they walked through the doors of my shop. Now, I simply stand at new doors. Different setting … same smiles!" A career that he had cherished ended, but he moved forward to a new job that brought a similar sense of personal satisfaction. He learned from the past he loved in order to construct and embrace a future that he could love, as well.

～～

Tuck away these suggestions to help you make the commitment to love life, to find in each new stage of life sources of joy and satisfaction:

Time rushes by; do not waste it.

Surprises often wait around the next corner; do not give up on the future because of the past.

Approach life with a positive outlook. Yes, you have suffered losses, but that means there were once also gains. If you've experienced blessings and joys before, what makes you think they will not come again? The emptiness of "what is no longer" calls forth the memory of "what was," and that is a glass-half-full equation. Put another way, focus on the reality that if happiness once existed, it can exist again (albeit in a new form).

Learn from yesterday for the purpose of constructing a new and happy tomorrow. Yes, the best may be yet to come. Yes, new joys may wait around the next corner. But we usually must take some actions to be open to and aware of those joys, to actually see them and appropriate them in our daily lives.

5. LOVE YOURSELF.

If others discern that you do not love yourself, they will assume you know something they do not and will, thus, be less likely to offer you love.

Remember that part of self-love is doing what's required to give yourself the gift of a bright future. Adopt the mantra, "I will not close the door on tomorrow because of yesterday."

There are a multitude of stories illustrating this principle. One of my favorites is about the late Harland Sanders (aka Colonel Sanders of KFC). Google "Harland Sanders" and you will find almost two hundred thousand entries! In other words, his has become a household name whether your house is in Kentucky, the Caribbean, or China. Read any of those two hundred thousand articles that you wish, and you are likely to find the same story of a man who loved to cook but lost his opportunity when a state road closed down the little service station café he operated. He settled into an undesired retirement on a Social Security pension of barely over $100 a month. But he loved to cook—especially chicken. So he began to visit restaurants, cooking his chicken on the premises and asking the owners to enter into a partnership with him. Legend (and a large number of corroborating reports) has it that he was turned down by over one thousand restaurateurs before someone finally said yes to his dream. The rest, as they say, is history. He would not let a loss from the past block his dreams for the future.

Sanders's love was cooking (particularly, frying chicken). Your passion may be something different. But whatever love has brought you joy in your yesterdays, do not allow its loss to close the door on your tomorrows. Learn from the experience of past love, assess what there was about it that provided meaning and joy, and use that knowledge in constructing a future with potential to bring new excitement and satisfaction.

Love yourself enough to be reasonable. I have often advised my children that in a world of over seven billion people, it is patently illogical to believe that there is only one person who can be the "true love" of their lives. That has always proven to be particularly timely advice whenever one of them has gone through the undesired breakup of a relationship. Simple reason attests that no one person, job, town, house, or anything else is likely to occupy so lofty a status as to be one's only "true love." And, as already noted in this chapter, to deny oneself new love actually dishonors the love(s) that went before.

~~~

I met my wife, Page, after the death of her first husband. He died in an untimely fashion as a young man, leaving a wife and two small daughters behind. Had Page's first marriage been a painful or fundamentally negative experience, she would have been far less open to the possibility of a new relationship. However, because love existed in the first marriage, she was aware that love can exist and that, for her, being married made life more complete than it would be if she remained single. To a certain extent, it was the positive nature of the first relationship that made possible her confidence in exploring a new relationship. She was aware that love exists, that relationships can occur, and that there is no one person who for all time can occupy all the space of an individual's heart. The human heart is a remarkable thing, almost accordion-like in its capacity to enlarge sufficiently to receive, welcome, and enjoy numerous sources of life and love.

So love yourself. Love yourself enough to believe in and work toward the future and enough to be reasonable, admitting that no one lost love will be the only love you can ever (or should ever) experience.

6. LIFE IS FLUID, NOT STAGNANT.

It moves in a forward direction, and those who are fully alive have no choice but to move with it. *Leave It to Beaver* reruns may reflect (however accurately or inaccurately) an epoch of history that nostalgic souls might wish to revisit. But the world has moved on from those years that the show portrayed. Life is fluid. It moves forward. So live by the wisdom of the words "carpe diem." Seize the day. Love freely and fully in the now, never assuming that "in time" you will get around to loving.

Charles Dickens was one of English literature's greatest authors. Whether or not it was his best work, probably none of his other stories have ever been cherished more or remembered longer than *A Christmas Carol*. Everyone who owns a television set has seen it (whether starring Alistair Sim, George C. Scott, Michael Caine, Patrick Stewart, or a host of others). We all know the story of Ebenezer Scrooge, the Cratchit family, and the ghosts who came calling on Christmas Eve. Thus, we all are also aware of Dickens' beautiful insights about love lost and found, insights made visible through the sudden and unexpected self-revelations experienced by Mr. Scrooge.

～～～

Remember the pain old Ebenezer felt when the Ghost of Christmas Past took him back to Fezziwig's house where he saw a Christmas party from his younger days? He had forgotten how wonderful it was to laugh and dance. He had forgotten how beautiful Fezziwig's daughter, Belle, was or how much he had loved her (and she him), and how painful it was to have lost her because of his lust for money. Ultimately, the scene was too emotionally excruciating for Scrooge to bear. He had gained things at the expense of love. He had gained money at the expense of relationship. He had gained a bank account at the expense of life. And he could not go back and retrieve that which was lost. He could not return and make Belle love him again. There had been a day when Scrooge believed he would get around to loving, that its time would come once other things had been fully addressed. But that night, accompanied by a ghost and its unwelcome dose of reality, Scrooge realized that life is fluid. It moves forward. And when we miss chances to love (whatever the object of that love may be), those precise chances do not often occur again. Carpe diem! Seize the day while it is at hand!

But the classic Christmas novel does not end there. Scrooge is also given tours of insight by the ghosts of Christmases present and yet to come. He sees how his greed destroys the people in its path, and he sees how love alone ultimately brings meaning to life. Thus, Scrooge awakens with a truly converted perspective on what living can be. Dickens says that from that day on, no one "kept Christmas" with more joy or enthusiasm than the former miser. Tiny Tim, whose death due to poverty was predicted by the Ghost of Christmas Future, did not die. Instead, Scrooge's generosity provided the medical and nutritional care that poverty had previously kept out of reach. Laughter took the place of hostility. Grace overcame abusiveness. Expressing love helped the old man rediscover much of what he lost in years past.[26]

∿

The truth is that there are things we cannot control. Time flies. We wish that were not the case, but we have no power to make it otherwise. Loves come and go. We wish they would come and stay, but life is not constructed that way. Live long enough and you will lose things you value deeply. We wish we could hold on to that which we value *ad infinitum*, but no one in history has ever figured out how to do that, and it isn't likely that you or I will, either. To find joy, we are called upon to do what we can whenever we can to affirm and incorporate love in life. We are called upon to exercise what control we do, in fact, possess.

While walking through the tents and signs at Occupy Wall Street, I bumped into a man who was there to protest what has happened to the textile industry. For generations, his family had worked in that industry, but little by little the majority of textile jobs have been outsourced overseas. The mills that provided the livelihood that he and his

---

[26]   Charles Dickens, *A Christmas Carol* (London: Chapman and Hall, 1843).

extended family (as well as tens of thousands of others like them) had counted on had closed their doors. He was understandably hurt, frightened, and angry, and was there to demand that the powers-that-be do something to resurrect the textile industry in America. He said to me, "I am not here to overthrow the government. I am here simply to ask someone to let me work again!" There was pathos and pain in his voice and a sense of purpose in his eyes.

However, as I had made my way to the Occupy Wall Street settlement earlier, I passed by a restaurant with a sign in the window reading "Now Hiring." So a mental connection became obvious. Though the man who talked with me had little control over the status of the textile industry in America, he did have control over his own life and potential sources of income. He possessed the power to make choices. He could have walked fewer than two blocks to a business that was hiring, where he could have applied for work. Whereas he did not have the power to regain his desired job, he did possess the power to find a new job. Another option was to spend his time and energy advocating for corporate reform. He did have sufficient control over his life and actions to make that choice. What's more, whether or not his actions would result in the restoration of his former job, they could help create a new movement that will eventually open stateside doors for textile workers. He had three options: to do nothing, since there was a greater issue over which he had no control; to take a job, though it was not the job he preferred; or to challenge the controlling system as one voice among many hoping for eventual systemic changes. "No one can do everything, but everyone can do something."

Transpose that story from Occupy Wall Street to your street, your life, your soul, your psyche. Loss is inevitable. Some things pass that will not come again. We have no control over that. Our choice is either to succumb to despair because of those losses or to take action for the future, exercising whatever control we do have over our own lives, emotions, and destinies. We do have the choice to surrender to grief and bitterness or to choose renewal and hope. We do have the choice to remain stuck or to move forward. Though lost treasures are rarely reclaimed, new treasures can be found when we're willing to look for them. And the greatest treasure of all is love. Whatever else has come and gone, love always remains an option. We all have sufficient control of our lives to claim love, to choose love, to experience new or renewed love, and to pass love along. That much control we do have, and that is a key to discovering joy.

If you appreciate yesterday, then embrace today and learn from it, but do so while leaning into tomorrow. If you learned from lost loves, use those lessons to create even stronger loves in times yet to come. If love ever mattered, know that love still matters. Don't miss it. Don't put it off. Love life, people, and experiences with zest and passion, and life will love you back in return. Some occasional loves will conclude along the way. So be it. Other loves, given the chance, will step forward to fill the gaps.

EIGHT

THE BENEFIT OF UNREQUITED LOVE

W e concluded the preceding chapter by asserting that if you love life, life will love you back in return. That is undeniably true. Life will love lovers in return. That does not mean, however, that every specific individual will return the love you offer to him or her.

"The greatest joy in life is to love and be loved" is a sentiment expressed by so many poets and philosophers that it would defy logic to footnote them all. Certainly, they make a strong and valid point. But what if you only realize half the equation? Is there joy to be found in the act of loving, even if that love is unrequited?

Ask a cat owner about the inherent satisfaction of loving for the pure joy of it. To be sure, there is the occasional cat that is affectionate. I owned one once. But she was an exception. Most cats seem to exist with an understanding that affection is something you provide and they receive, not vice versa. Unlike dogs, who wag their tails and drool at the sight of an owner entering the room, cats are fiercely independent. They come and go as they please and seem perfectly satisfied if everyone else does likewise. They require (and seem to desire) precious little interaction, appearing primarily interested in your keeping their food bowl full and their litter box clean. And yet, it is not uncommon to read of someone who lives alone and finds companionship, fulfillment, and meaning in a house filled with cats. The acts of loving them and of caring for them bring rewards all their own. This indicates that there is a real and deep sense of joy to be experienced in the activity of loving, whether or not that love is equally or demonstrably reciprocated.

Parents of infants are quick to attest that they have never felt love so pronounced and profound as the love they feel for a new baby, despite the fact that the child merely takes with no initial concept of giving back in return. She cries. He demands to be fed, changed, rocked to sleep, and afforded attention to matter how late the hour or how tired the parent. The baby does not seem particularly worried that mom or dad cannot sleep. He or she does not seem concerned that mom and dad have busy lives outside the tasks associated with parenting. And pediatricians suggest that even the occasional smiles the child bestows upon adoring parents are sometimes just grimaces produced by gas. Nothing on earth is so dearly loved or is a source of such unparalleled joy as is that baby, even though the child is still too young to conceptualize love, much less to return it.

Years ago, when I worked for a time at a state hospital for people with profound mental and physical disabilities, I came to know a nurse who was employed there. The majority of the patients she served on a daily basis were developmentally incapable of saying "Thanks," let alone "I love you." And yet the nurse consistently turned down career advancement opportunities in order to remain their primary caregiver. How does one explain that? More than once I heard her say, "The more of myself I give to the powerless, the more true life is given to me." Hal and Sidra Stone, in their book *Embracing Each Other*, have this to say about loving that is not based on reciprocation: "Each relationship leaves behind an expanded consciousness and the gift of new or enhanced selves."[27]

∿∿

Meaning in life is often found by serving when there is little promise of being served, giving when there is little hope of receiving in return, and loving when there is little assurance that your love will be returned in kind. In truth, the central principle of this book is that life takes on its deepest meaning when all our decisions, words, and actions are predicated upon one single question: "Is this the loving thing to decide, say, or do?" The question should not be, "Will I receive love by following this course of action?" but rather, "Is this the loving course of action to take?" We simply can never be assured that by loving we will be loved in return. But ultimately, that is not the point. The point is that by loving, we will receive life in return. "Find love, find life!"

---

[27] Hal and Sidra Stone, op. cit., p. 68.

Consider the following ideas that support making active loving the central motivation in life, whether or not specific expressions of love are always reciprocated.

1. LOVE IS A PHILOSOPHY, NOT AN INVESTMENT.

It is an approach to living, a methodology of the heart for relating to others in the world. As such, it transcends the question "What's in it for me?"

Obviously, we all enjoy being loved and need to experience that. Numerous studies on this topic have been conducted involving pets and children (whether or not said studies can be justified ethically, especially by those who endorse the philosophy of active and consistent loving). Whereas the particulars vary slightly from test to test, most focus on the affirmation that comes via touch and voice and what happens when that affirmation is provided or denied. Study after study indicates that when everything else is equal (that is, all primary physical needs are met), the children and animals who grow and develop positively are the ones who receive physical and verbal affection. Those who are fed and sheltered but otherwise remain untouched and receive no verbal affirmation demonstrate stunted physical growth, emotional immaturity, and (in the case of very young animals, especially puppies) sometimes even death. To achieve proper self-actualization, we all need to receive love.

However, a fundamental need to receive love should not be our only priority. How shallow and self-absorbed it is to ponder, "If I offer an ounce of love, will I get an ounce back? Or better yet, a pound?" Loving as "investment" fails to live up to the definition of love. It becomes, instead, an act of narcissism (not a lovely thing at all).

One of the regrettable tendencies of the "Me" generation is the practice of taking self-love, which is a good thing, to a bad extreme. Author Jean Twenge rightly observes that "narcissists love themselves too much."[28] She illustrates that observation by referring to a school that went over the top in an effort to instill self-esteem in its students: "A preschool in Manhattan designated September as All About Me Month."[29] To instill a proper sense of self-worth is a healthy thing. To encourage people to adopt an "all about me" philosophy, however, builds a foundation that results in ultimate loneliness and interpersonal failure. Life is not "all about me," and those who choose to think it is have purchased a ticket to misery.

A fundamental sense of happiness comes by choosing to express and extend love, and can, in fact, be found in no other way at all. And that's the irony, isn't it? Love is a philosophy, not an investment. And yet, only those who adopt that philosophy can reap and enjoy the returns of happy and meaningful lives.

2. LOVE PLACES ME IN CHARGE OF MY OWN JOY.

I get to choose whether I will follow the road that leads to happiness. Usually a person who focuses principally on the meeting of his or her own needs winds up dissatisfied with life. Enough is never enough. Every accomplishment or acquisition is judged against that of someone else who seems to have accomplished or acquired more. Likewise, every loss or setback seems to be patently unfair, whether or not it is part of the normal course of human living. Those who focus too much on self condemn themselves to

---

[28] Jean M. Twenge, *The Narcissist Epidemic* (NY: Free Press, 2009), p.18.
[29] Ibid., p. 186.

discontent. If I have a proper and healthy sense of self-love, why would I choose to follow that path?

I choose, instead, to find joy. And a weight of opinion from philosophers, poets, theologians, and philanthropists across the ages says that joy is the property of those who love. As that nurse in the state hospital put it, "The more of myself I give … the more true life is given to me." Or, as Deepak Chopra writes, "If you want joy, give joy to others."[30] Statements attributed to Siddhartha, Mohammed, and Jesus add a loud "Amen!" to that. So do many attributed to Shakespeare and Browning (whether Elizabeth or Robert) and William James and Cole Porter and Mother Teresa, and the list goes on and on across the centuries. Find love, find life! Knowing that, why would I make a different choice? I desire life in its fullness, and if that which I desire comes essentially by loving, then by all means I choose to love!

Furthermore, this approach to life means that my joy is not "bestowed." I do not have to depend on someone or something else to provide it. By making my own decision to live life according to the principle of active loving, I am free to choose joy, not to wait for it to be given to me. I can find happiness in tending the cat or cuddling the baby who may or may not wish (or be able) to reciprocate. I can be the nurse to developmentally disabled people who cannot say "Thanks," and I can find meaning in so doing. I can even forgive someone who has not requested forgiveness or, perhaps, does not even acknowledge needing it. Regardless, I can release the burden of resentment that I carried and can, in so doing, choose joy. "Forgiveness is a key to happiness. Inner peace can be reached only when [it is] practiced."[31]

---

[30] Deepak Chopra, *The Seven Spiritual Laws of Success* (San Rafael, CA: Amber-Allen Publishing, 1994), p. 30.

[31] Jampolsky, op. cit., p. 65.

I can focus upon the beauties that existed within a relationship that the other person ended, even though I had hoped it would endure. The love, laughter, and life inherent in my memories are things the other person cannot take away. They are mine to retain and to enjoy, even though "what was" is no longer "what shall remain."

You and I can love people for who they are or were, even if they are not particularly lovable. Most of the genuinely gifted people I have ever known have a sense of grace, even humility, about them. On occasion, however, we all bump into people who fit Ms. Twenge's description of narcissism. Two encounters come to mind. The first was with one of the world's greatest sopranos, and the second was with one of the twentieth century's most acclaimed comics.

༔

I encountered the first following a performance. I complimented her voice, and she smiled. But while receiving my compliment, she rudely dismissed a young person who stepped forward to ask for an autograph. I was a source of affirmation. The young man, no less affirming, was perceived as a mere inconvenience.

The comedian shared a plane ride with me to Denver, Colorado. He told amusing stories, and I responded with laughter and appreciation. However, when a passenger seated nearby told a story that was clearly funny, and when several people laughed in approval, the comedian grew silent and sullen. He was not prepared to share the spotlight. He perceived another's humor as a threat to his own.

Both the singer and the comedian seemed primarily interested in being recognized and appreciated. They came across as arrogant and even condescending. Each appeared too much taken with self and too little aware of neighbor. However, my experience of their personalities in those given moments in time does nothing to lessen my appreciation for their abilities. I love to hear her sing. I love to allow him to make me laugh. I choose to love what they do because that choice brings me joy. Lingering on the negative memory would serve no positive purpose for me. Maybe their actions were temporarily out of character. Maybe they were overly tired. Maybe I encountered them in a bad moment. Ultimately, none of that matters. What matters is the choice I make about them, and I choose to receive beauty from one and laughter from the other. I can choose to love what they do, even if they are not always entirely lovable. In so doing, I exercise the freedom to choose happiness.

～～～

If happiness can be bestowed, it can also be denied because it is the property of someone or something else. However, if my choice to live lovingly is the source of my happiness, then it is my property, and I can own and celebrate it regardless of any outside influence. That, I think, is at least part of what Judith Orloff, a professor of psychiatry at UCLA, must have had in mind when she wrote, "Today, go on a compassion spree. Put no holds on your heart or how you'll love others."[32] As a psychiatrist, her goal is to help people find meaning, peace, and satisfaction. Obviously, she understands and attests that we find those things by choosing to love. Go on a compassion spree! Happiness is yours to choose. No one else can provide it, nor can they take it away. Live by the principle of active loving whether or not that love is returned, and you will have chosen the path to joy.

[32] Judith Orloff, *Emotional Freedom* (NY: Harmony Books, 2009), p. 373.

3. LOVE, EVEN WHEN UNRECIPROCATED, BROADENS MY SENSE OF SELF.

LOVE HELPS CLARIFY VALUES.

By immersing myself in the activity of conscious, daily loving, I determine what that value is. I discern via a disciplined daily practice of love that life brings meaning. It is satisfying and fulfilling. There's more happiness now than there was when other values were core. If I can recall a time when I was primarily motivated by a commitment to self, I realize now that my sense of self is in fact enhanced by being primarily committed to love. If I can recall a time when I thought satisfaction was located in power, prestige, or possessions, I realize now that having given myself over to the daily discipline of active loving, I am far more satisfied than I was previously.

This is not to say that there are no further concerns for self. Self-love is a vital part of the life of loving. Neither is it to say that there is no more desire for accomplishments or acquisitions. It is simply to say that when love becomes the core value of my life, then everything else is interpreted in light of that. And thus, everything else can be radically reprioritized and properly appreciated. I am no longer possessed by my possessions. I am no longer held captive by the image I think the world expects or demands of me. I am no longer dictated by other people's definitions of what it means to succeed or be whole. I have established my own system of values, a system based upon life's preeminent virtue, and thus my sense of self is broader and deeper and more substantive than it could possibly otherwise be.

LOVE REMINDS US THAT WE HAVE AN INHERENT CAPACITY TO LOVE.

Having once known what love is like, and the joy and richness associated with it, I am aware that I have the capacity to experience and express love. Though a particular love may not have lasted *ad infinitum*, I still know that I have loved and, therefore, can love again.

~~~

At dinner recently, my wife and I were introduced to a young novelist not long removed from a six-year relationship with a man she thought would become her husband. After six years of monogamous commitment to each other, he became unsure of the relationship and its future and, thus, said goodbye. Though one might expect her to relate a tale of woe and tears, she surprised us by saying, "I learned a lot from that relationship. Parts of it are already forming the basis of my next novel, so I guess I owe him. But let me tell you what I appreciate most about him. He came along after I had lost the one I thought was the man of my dreams. At that critical juncture, he taught me that I could love again. That's what I owe him for most of all. That insight was his great gift to me. I can love again ... and I will!" She paused for a moment, then smiled and added one brief statement, perfectly crafted in a novelist's style: "Next time will be e ven better."

Having loved, even having loved and lost, broadens our sense of self by assuring us that we possess the capacity to love. And that includes the capacity to love again. Sometimes when "again" comes around, there is the serendipity of realizing that this time is even better.

LOST LOVES, OVER THE COURSE OF TIME, ASSURE US OF THE REALITY OF EMOTIONAL HEALING.

"I cannot live without her!" we protest, but somehow we do live. "My life will end if he leaves me!" we cry, but somehow life does not end. The human spirit has remarkable powers of resiliency and regeneration. We are equipped to heal.

Given enough time, we realize that life does go on and so, in fact, do we. It is different. There may be regrets, but there are also happy memories. There may be pain, but there are also lessons we learned from pain that cannot be learned quite as effectively from any other source. And whether or not we imagined it would happen, the sun does rise again on the morning after heartbreak, and on the morning after that, and the one after that. We go on. Things are not the same. But we journey toward and eventually discover a "new normal." Sometimes the journey is slow, awkward, lonely, and difficult. But the journey still proceeds. There are occasional moments of relapse into despondency and tears, but those moments become less and less frequent with the passage of time. And somewhere along the pilgrimage to wholeness, we find ourselves singing with Gloria Gaynor, "I will survive!" And eventually that lyric changes to "I did survive, in spite of it all!"

Having experienced love, even love that did not last, empowers us to make choices based on a personal philosophy of life as opposed to cultural pressures.

We can choose to disregard well-intended but poorly-thought-out advice, like, "Just be thankful that you had love once. So many people never do," or "Maybe you should just throw yourself into your work," or "You married for love the first time. Next time, just marry for companionship," or other pieces of counsel that, having loved, you will be wise enough to ignore. Your philosophy of life will dictate a different approach, one that embraces fresh starts, second chances, and the power of will: "I chose to love, and now I choose to love again."

Recognizing that personal enrichment comes from the discipline of loving, we make choices based on that experience despite the world counseling us to make other choices. For example, we choose to forgive. The world may say, "Don't get mad, get even," but having experienced the burden of grudge bearing and also the liberation of loving, we are empowered to make the wise choice to forgive.[33] We choose to give to those who cannot repay the favor. The world may say, "Each investment should bring a return," but having experienced the unparalleled joy that comes from helping those who cannot help themselves, we are empowered to make the choice to assist others, understanding that the certain return is joy. Living by the discipline of active loving equips us to make choices based on a personal philosophy rather than cultural pressures. And the choices we make, when motivated by the will to love, consistently lead to happiness.

Even when a particular love ends, it does not denigrate the good that existed before it ended nor the lessons and memories that are cherished afterward.

My mother's first cousin played ten years of baseball as a catcher in the major leagues (and one season was the starting catcher for the American League All-Star team).

---

[33]　Ibid., p. 348. A research study from Stanford University states that practicing forgiveness decreases stress, anger, and psychosomatic symptoms.

Those years were the happiest of his life. Some folks, following retirement, live with a sense of loss and sadness. A bit of that is to be expected and understood if a person enjoyed his or her work. However, my mother's cousin never exhibited grief at the end of his career. For the rest of his life, he relished the friendships and memories of that career. He was not trapped by the past but instead maintained a full and busy post-retirement life. And yet, whenever asked to recount his experiences, he would regale people with story after story of his trips on the road, the best pitchers he ever caught or faced, the best hitters he ever knew, and what it was like to catch a full nine innings in the All-Star game. It was obvious to everyone that he enjoyed the stories as much as anybody who listened to them, if not more. Those stories comprised his emotional scrapbook. He owned those memories and could take them out and enjoy them when he chose. And when the last inning closed on the final chapter of his career, it did not take away from him any of the memories or experiences that had gone before.

∽

The victim of divorce may lose a partner he or she had counted on for the long haul, but the person who left does not have power to take the good memories along with them. One still possesses the memories of courtship and young love, of getting married and starting a family, of the laughter and passion and joy that preceded the concluding days when joy was diminished.

Lost loves can become the textbooks of life, memory manuscripts that we can recall and examine, extracting lessons like, "This brought me happiness," "This brought me sadness," "That season of life was delightful, and here are the reasons why," and "That period was stressful, and here are the components of it that I will be alert enough to avoid in future relationships." When love ends, the goodness that existed in a relationship and the lessons we learned from it are not extinguished.

4. LOVE IS A LASTING VALUE THAT PROVIDES A POSITIVE LEGACY.

People well-remembered are rarely recalled for being loved but rather for loving. And the more love a person offers, the greater the legacy that person creates. It doesn't matter if some loves were truncated along the way. It matters instead that the person is remembered as having a consistently loving nature.

Death is one of life's few inevitabilities. And we all die poor. As the saying goes, "No one ever saw a U-Haul on the back of a hearse!" Thus, the question that has priority should not be "What riches can I attain?" but instead, "What can I do with my life that enriches both myself and others?" How we live, not what we have, creates our legacy.

How much money did Mother Teresa leave in the bank? Or Martin Luther King, Jr.? Or Gandhi? Or Nelson Mandela? They are remembered not for what they acquired, but rather for what they gave away. Primarily, they are remembered as people who gave the gift of love.

Of course, one might ask, "Why should I be concerned about a legacy? Once I'm gone, I'm gone." The answer is that by living a life devoted to the discipline of loving, once you're gone, you're not gone! Love becomes the essence of you (put another way, the essential you) which lives on in the memories of others touched by your loving nature and in the commitment to loving that others made because of your influence. One of the great chefs in Los Angeles confessed, "Most of the recipes that I use were my mother's. She taught me how to cook, how to balance flavors, how to inject a creative flair without compromising the integrity of the dish. So though she has been deceased for eighteen years, every time I open my restaurant, she is directing things in the kitchen." Her influence lives on in the life of another person profoundly touched by that influence.

How many good and decent people do you know who are the products of good and decent parents? How many actors can name a high school drama coach whose encouragement turned them on to the craft? How many professional athletes can name a Little League coach who did the same? Success breeds success. Talent inspires talent. And love keeps on loving even after the original source of that love has gone.

Some things do last forever. They last beyond the people who initiated them. Those of us who were touched by their influence offer to others what we received from them. In that sense, the ones who loved and influenced us keep on loving and influencing others through us.

Historians note that sitting presidents in second terms try to craft their legacies. While managing the arduous daily tasks of governing, something psychological occurs that causes them to take up an additional mantle, to champion a cause not as clearly championed in their first term. Whether consciously or subconsciously, they try to determine the way they will be remembered. Others do so after leaving office. Perhaps the most notable illustration of that in recent times is the life of former president Jimmy Carter. Whatever one's opinions of his years in the White House may be, it is hard to argue the myriad contributions he has made to the world following his tenure as president. One of the ways he will be longest remembered is for his tireless work with Habitat for Humanity. Carter is the first to confess that the late Millard Fuller, Habitat's founder, lives on through him and through others like him. And both Fuller and Carter will continue to live on for generations to come through all who embrace that mission as their own.

~~~

As the years pass, the question of how one wishes to be remembered becomes an emotionally-pressing subject. Whether or not you have a belief in life beyond this life, it is indisputable that each person lives on in the influence he or she leaves behind. Do you want your influence to be positive and productive, to bring smiles and emulation, to make the world a better and brighter place? If so, the surest way to achieve such a legacy is to build your life on the daily discipline of loving. Live each day with three questions in mind as you conduct your life's business:

1. Is this the loving thing to say?

2. Is the loving thing to do?

3. Will this add to or detract from the presence of love in the world?

Consistently ask just those three questions with a determination to proceed from a platform of love, and your influence will help create a climate of joy that will live on after your life is concluded. It does not matter if all of your decisions to love are returned in kind. Whether or not your acts of love are reciprocated is not the issue. The point is that you will have made this world a more loving place.

Following his death, quotes from the late Steve Jobs began to circulate in the news and on the Internet. One of the most poignant was, "Being the richest man in the cemetery doesn't matter to me … Going to bed at night saying that we've done something wonderful … that's what matters to me."[34] His words resonate with those who are truly wise. And for those who want to go to bed at night knowing they have done something truly wonderful, you can't beat loving!

5. TO BASE MY LIFE ON THE ACTIVITY OF LOVING, WHETHER OR NOT THAT LOVE IS CONSISTENTLY RETURNED IN KIND, MEANS THAT I HAVE LIVED FOR A NOBLE PURPOSE.

A wise spiritual writer of almost two thousand years ago observed that when all the splendid virtues of life are placed side by side, the greatest of these is love.

A woman who was once internationally known as a successful model made an interesting observation. She confessed, "I have always been valued for how I look. It's the only thing that mattered. What people saw on the outside is what counted in my life. It was my only contribution." After a rather pregnant pause, she continued, "But the years change what people see on the outside. And in time, only that which is shining through from the inside can be construed as true beauty." Apparently that woman has as much inner depth as she has outer beauty.

---

[34] Steve Jobs, quoted in *The Wall Street Journal*, May 25, 1993.

∼∼∼

Ultimately, our lives will be defined by actions more than acquisitions, by motives more than material goods, by personality more than power, by altruism more than authority, by mercy more than might, by service more than self-indulgence, by friendship more than fashion, and by love more than anything else at all. If you consciously say to yourself, "I will live each day with love as my primary motivation," you will be a person of beauty. And your beauty, observed by those whose lives you touch, will not be based upon fashion, complexion, the color of your hair, or the size of your waist. As the model said, the years change all that. Why not aspire for beauty that is changeless? To do so simply means adopting the commitment to live by the philosophy of active loving.

It must be noted that making the decision to love on a daily basis is not an easy commitment to maintain. People and forces will rise up as considerable challenges to that commitment. Not everyone or everything make loving easy. Many people and situations, instead, make it one of life's most daring tests. Rejection and fatigue become roadblocks to loving. A lack of appreciation does likewise. The same is true for the uneasy feeling that the world makes us doormats, that gentle equals vulnerable, or that nice guys finish last. It takes strength to love. It requires hard work and a daily renewal of devotion to the effort. But, in the end, there is no more virtuous or meaningful way to live. And every challenge met results in deeper peace and joy than we had known before or ever dreamed of knowing. It is an uphill journey some of the time, but a journey toward a life of inner satisfaction that is available on no other highway.

If you commit yourself to a daily discipline of active loving, you will have signed on not merely to live in support of, but indeed to become one with life's most noble virtue. The world's true heroes have always understood that.

Love is its own reward. To be loved is always a source of joy. There is no doubt about that. But at the end of the day, the activity of loving is a deeper and more lasting source. It is something we own, and no one else can take away. We are in control of our own choices at that point, and the choices we make bring happiness, power, and peace. So reciprocation, though wonderful, is ultimately not the point. Joy is. And it comes to us through the act of loving even more than it does through the experience of being loved.

THE CHALLENGE OF
SELF-LOVE

*Self-love, my liege, is not so vile a sin
as self-neglecting.*[1]

-William Shakespeare, *King Henry V*

From the outset, we have contended that love is a decision we make followed by actions we take on behalf of others. In the preceding chapter, we sought to establish a rationale supporting the conviction that love, even when not reciprocated, is its own reward. We love for the pure joy of loving. All of that is true. But it should also be noted that appropriate love of self is also part of the mix of creating a life based on the discipline of active loving. In fact, many contend that those who do not properly love themselves are fundamentally unable to fully love others.

---

1   William Shakespeare, *King Henry V*, Act 2, Scene 4.

The first Buddha said, "You must love yourself before you love another. By accepting yourself and fully being what you are, your simple presence can make others happy."[35] The same is true, of course, when it comes to receiving love or even believing that love is being extended to us. Michael Keaton's character of Riggan Thomson in the movie *Birdman* struggles to accept, affirm, believe in, and love himself. As the film progresses, it is clear that no amount of affirmation from others can compensate for his deep feelings of guilt, self-doubt, and insecurity. In short, until he learns to love himself, he is unable to fully accept love from anyone else. That's part of the wisdom in the words, "You shall love your neighbor as yourself."

Note, of course, that love of self must be "appropriate." Self-indulgence is not that. Nor are self-absorption or self-aggrandizement, egocentrism, or greed. Self-love implies a correct understanding of self vis-à-vis the world.

∿

A woman described her brother-in-law as "the most self-centered man alive." I responded that such is quite a statement, and I wondered what made her feel that way. She answered my inquiry with a story. The preceding summer she, her husband, and their children had joined her brother and sister and their family in sharing a beach house for a week's vacation. The first night there, the families sat together and watched television. In the course of the evening, a documentary was presented about the results of a tsunami in Japan. The pictorial evidence of human suffering was indescribable.

---

[35]   A quote attributed to Hindu Prince Gautama Siddharta, the first Buddha.

The next morning at breakfast the brother-in-law said, "I had a hard time sleeping last night." Another relative quickly replied, "So did I. I couldn't get those awful images out of my head." The brother-in-law answered, "What images?" When the response was made that the troubling images in question were those of the tsunami victims in Japan, he replied, "Oh no, I wasn't thinking of that. Yesterday when we were driving down here, I heard a clicking noise in my car engine. I don't know what it is, but with my luck, it will be expensive! I worried about it all night." The images of tens of thousands of people whose homes, possessions, and, in some cases, loved ones had been washed out to sea did not cost him a wink of sleep. But fear that he might be facing an unexpected auto expense caused him to toss and turn all night long. His concern, even in the face of the massive needs of others, was all about himself. That is not proper self-love. That is, instead, self-centeredness. Those are two different things.

~~~

A proper sense of self-love does not disparage the needs and rights of others. It simply confesses that all individuals have needs and rights that must be taken seriously, and that includes self as well as neighbor. "You yourself, as much as anybody else in the entire universe, deserve your love and affection."[36] How can we take care of ourselves, so that we will be fully equipped to love the world around us?

Let's consider just a brief handful of suggestions.

---

[36] *Ibid.*, Prince Gautama.

1. SELF-LOVE REQUIRES SELF-AWARENESS.

I must know who I am, what my talents and interests are, what my personality type is (and what that says about me), and how all that is, in fact, of value.

Across the years I have heard numerous individuals confess that they assess themselves against others. They compare and contrast. Whereas we learn valuable lessons by observing the lives and activities of exemplary people, we diminish the quality of our own existence if we think we have to match or exceed their qualities and accomplishments. You will always be able to locate someone who is taller or slimmer or richer or prettier or more famous or more powerful or younger or a more accomplished singer or artist or cook or whatever else it is that you think is desirable. And if the success of another makes you define your own life as a failure, then you will forever be a failure because there will forever be another who has exceeded your threshold in this or that. In Gregory Maguire's novel, *Confessions of an Ugly Stepsister*, an artist speaks to Iris, the stepsister of the beautiful Clara. The artist says, "Self-mockery is an uglier thing than any human face."[37] If we define ourselves over against the outward strengths of others, we will forever feel inadequate because we will always be able to locate a Clara simply by searching diligently enough. Others serve well as examples, models, and sources of inspiration. But it is foolish, sometimes even emotionally suicidal, to allow anyone else to set the bar on what success or self-actualization means for us. And the irony is that sometimes, unbeknownst to us, the one we envy envies us.

---

[37] Gregory Maguire, *Confessions of an Ugly Stepsister* (NY: Harper, 1999), p. 178.

Some time ago, one of the finest and most beloved screen actors in America was in conversation with a friend of mine who is an accomplished public speaker. My friend confessed to me that he was a bit star-struck when he visited the actor's home and saw the photos, the awards, and an Oscar statue on the shelves. Partway through their visit, the actor said to my friend, "You know, I really envy you. I can perform someone else's script on film, but for the life of me I can't write a speech or stand up in front of a live audience and deliver it. I'm probably the worst public speaker I know. I wish I had your talent." My friend said it was all he could do not to fall out of his chair. He was sitting in the beautiful home of an Oscar-winning actor, a man of undeniable gifts, skills, and acclaim. But the actor felt inadequate against the abilities of his guest. My friend said to me, "It was quite shocking to realize that someone I envied, in fact, envied me."

If we knew the other person's heart, we might realize such is not infrequently the case. External accomplishments are not the final measure by which the value of a life is assessed. Many who have countless such external accomplishments understand that. Some still have a sense that something is missing, that the joy or peace they see in you is something they wish they had for themselves. Self-awareness, therefore, means at least this much: that my gifts are my gifts, and they are not lessened in quality by observing someone else who appears to have more gifts. In truth, I cannot get within the skin of that other person, therefore I cannot know whether or not that person is as gifted as appearance suggests or as happy as I assume. My task is simply to confess, celebrate, and employ my own strengths and talents and find the joy that is inherent in doing so.

~~~

Malcolm Gladwell reminds us in *Outliers* of the brilliant physicist J. Robert Oppenheimer as a young man. Oppenheimer was described by those who knew him as impractical and ill-equipped for most endeavors of life. A scientist at UC Berkeley said of him: "He couldn't run a hamburger stand!" That statement was probably true. However, he discovered what he was able to do well and he did it, becoming one of the most accomplished (albeit controversial) figures in the world of physics in the twentieth century.[38] A healthy state of self-awareness involves discovering what we can do, however those talents may compare or contrast with anyone else's, and then doing it.

A helpful suggestion for attaining healthy self-awareness is to discard these three burdensome words from our vocabulary: should, ought, and must. "I really should do this since everyone I respect seems to enjoy doing it." "I really ought to be better at that activity if I am to have a meaningful life." "I must develop a keener sense of this or that if my life is to have value." Really? Says who? Just as my gifts are my gifts, so my tastes are my tastes. Not enjoying the things that appeal to you in no way lessens my worth as a human being, just as your worth is not reduced because you do not share all my interests or passions.

For years I feared I lacked sophistication because I do not enjoy opera. I love music. I love theater. One would think, therefore, that opera would be a natural passion for me. It isn't. "Certainly," I convinced myself, "if I am to be a person of acceptable refinement, I must develop a taste for opera." I made the effort, albeit a somewhat modest

---

[38] Malcolm Gladwell, *Outliers: The Story of Success* (NY: Little, Brown and Company, 2008), p. 99.

one. Every foray into a concert hall to see an opera was like taking a triple dose of Ambien. It was not that I didn't get it. It was that I didn't like it. The truth is that I had no desire to "get it." For me, going to an enjoyable concert meant hearing James Taylor, Joni Mitchell, or John Legend, rather than the songs of Don Giovanni or La Bohème. I simply could not cross the musical horizon to what I assumed was the land of sophistication on the other side.

Then one evening I had dinner in the home of one of the great baritones of contemporary opera, a man who has shared top billing with Plácido Domingo and others of similar status. As soon as I entered his den, I recognized the track that was playing on his stereo system. It was a song by Emmylou Harris. I said, "I have that same number on a CD. But the rendition I have is a duet by Willie Nelson and Merle Haggard." My host immediately reached into a shelf filled with hundreds of CDs and produced the one I had mentioned. The man owns the largest collection of American folk and country music I have ever seen. "It's what I listen to for personal pleasure," he said as he casually filled our wine glasses for dinner. He, a renowned operatic singer, enjoys Emmylou, Willie, and Merle. Suddenly I decided it was permissible to throw out the concept of "musical must" as it related to my sense of self-esteem. No more would I say I "must" develop different musical tastes if I wish to be sophisticated. Although I still occasionally listen to opera (rarely by choice), I am very much at home with my own musical preferences. They are neither better nor worse than someone else's. They are simply mine. As Duke Ellington once said in response to a question regarding what defines good music, "It's whatever sounds good to you." Self-awareness that leads to self-acceptance is a liberating thing.

All of this is not to say that we shouldn't stretch ourselves, that we cannot grow, or that we should become satisfied with a personal status quo. Having a sense of adventure in life requires trying new things and opening ourselves to new experiences. However, at the end of the day we are who we are, and we should never feel apologetic about that. If we were all cookie-cutter imitations of one another, neat and tidy little Stepford automatons, what a boring world it would be. Self-love requires self-awareness, which hopefully will lead to self-acceptance.

2. SELF-LOVE REQUIRES SELF-FORGIVENESS.

As Gerald Jampolsky reminds us, "It is important to be gentle with yourself."[39]

Guilt takes the life out of life perhaps more than any of the other human emotions. Often the guilt is unearned; it is instead simply a reminder that we have tried to live in a way consistent with the imposed values of others but not in a way that actually reveals a lack of ethics or integrity. Even if we have reason for feeling guilty, having transgressed indisputable boundaries of right and wrong, guilt, at most, should serve to educate and equip us in order that we will make more appropriate and acceptable choices in the future. It should not prompt a self-imposed lifetime sentence of remorse. Do you feel guilty about an experience from the past? If so, then assess it (by asking, "Should it reasonably bring guilt?"), take actions if possible to right any actual wrong, learn the lessons it has to teach, and then discard it and move on.

---

[39] Jampolsky, op. cit., p. 39.

There should be a single standard of behavioral expectations. A suitable standard would be, "Is this a loving thing to do or say?" If there is a single standard, then it is both inappropriate and unfair to hold any individual to a higher or stricter standard than anyone else. Thus, whereas I should not expect more of you than I do of myself, I likewise have no right to expect more of myself than I do of you. If I think forgiveness should apply for whatever errors may exist in your past, then simple logic decrees that same forgiveness should be available to me (and to all).

~~~

One of the most devoted clergymen I know told me of an experience with a staff member who worked for him several years ago. He (the minister) had always expected himself to be a virtually flawless example of moral living in the public eye. When he went through a divorce, he was burdened with a sense of guilt. People, he believed, had expected better of him. Surely, he feared, they now viewed him as a failure, perhaps even as a fraud. Thus did he limp his way from one day to the next, trying to maintain an acceptable level of work performance while struggling to keep his emotional head above water. All who knew him realized that he was not succeeding at either of those efforts.

One day a young woman on his staff walked into his office unannounced. She spoke didactically and with a sense of authority bordering on frustration. "Do you judge your church members for experiencing failure in their daily lives?" she asked.

He answered, "Of course not. It's not my job to judge. I just try to help people. It's all about grace."

She stepped forward, no more than a foot away from him, looked straight into his eyes and said, "What right do you have to withhold grace from yourself and then presume you understand it well enough to offer it to anyone else?"

He told me that moment was his epiphany. "How could I tell others about fresh starts and second chances," he said, "if I denied those things to myself?"

~~~

Have you dropped the ball in ways large or small in times past? Of course you have. We all have. One thing is for certain: You cannot rewrite history. You cannot undo the ill-advised things that you did in your yesterdays. But you can take action to prevent those yesterdays, and their memories, from imprisoning you emotionally.

If you need to offer an apology, offer it. Make the call, send a letter, write the e-mail, do whatever you need to do. Whether or not the apology is accepted is not the issue. If you need to apologize, you find freedom from ongoing guilt in simply taking that step. Once done, there's nothing else you can do, and the matter resides with another.

If you need to talk with a trained listener, schedule time with a counselor or clergy. Carl Jung wrote that "as soon as humans were capable of conceiving the idea of sin, they had recourse to psychic concealment—or, to put it in analytical language, repressions arose."[40] And repression is deadly. Remember this: when bad things are buried, they grow bigger! If you are unable on your own to release a sense of guilt, find someone who can help you do so. Otherwise the

---

[40] Carl G. Jung, *Modern Man in Search of a Soul* (San Diego: Harcourt, Inc., 1933), p. 31.

guilt will grow bigger, possessing the potential to consume you, or, at least, to rob you of any possibility for joy.

If you experience guilt, learn the lessons it has to teach. What did you do or leave undone that brings you pain? What motivated you to take said action or not to act? If you are convinced you did the wrong thing, what does the memory say about your priorities then and how they should be adjusted now? What different values would be more appropriate motivators in the future?

A man whose marriage ended due to his relentless personal work ethic (resulting in his wife's feeling abandoned by him) could not subsequently convince her to give him a second chance. After their marriage ended, he went through a season of guilt. However, he was intelligent enough to use such as a tool for self-discernment. Later he shared with me the personal insight that period of guilt and discernment provided: "I cannot correct my first mistake. But I can reflect on it so that the next time around the mistake is not repeated." Voilà! If you experience guilt, then learn the lessons it has to teach so that past mistakes will not be repeated in the future. Do not, however, allow that guilt to impair or preclude the future you deserve. That is to fail twice.

Perhaps simplest and most important of all: let it go. Time moves on. Be emotionally intelligent enough to do likewise. The great spirit of life—call it God, wisdom, charity, creativity, or anything else—is less interested in where we've been than in where we're going. Life authentically lived is never inert. It is never about sitting still. And trying to move forward without resolving guilt is like trying to run a marathon with a ball and chain attached your leg. It simply cannot be done, at least not with any reasonable effectiveness. We are all mortal, flesh and blood. We all make mistakes. It is inevitable. The best and most ethical person you have ever known, if honest, would quickly confess that he or she remembers and can name numerous moments of errors in judgment and behavior. What makes those people admirable and wise is that they do not allow themselves to be defined by those moments. Instead they learn from them, forgive themselves, let go, and move on.

3. SELF-LOVE INVOLVES TAKING APPROPRIATE CARE OF BODY AND MIND.

For a number of years my wife, Page, owned and operated a business called Body-Mind, Inc. It was a training center for people wanting to get in shape, to achieve increased physical health, to counteract the effects of arthritis, aging, mastectomies, or cardiovascular issues. The training center employed a variety of methods, from Pilates reformers to Gyrotonic towers to numerous other approaches aimed at maintaining or restoring physical well-being. The title of the business came from Page's commitment that the health of body and mind are inextricably related. She believes (and reports from her clients have corroborated this) that increased physical conditioning results in increased emotional well-being. I often tell people that wherever their bodies go, their emotions go with them.

I confess to being a "foodie." I love the tastes and textures of foods. I love how things smell when cooking. I enjoy creating new dishes and experimenting, asking, "Will this seasoning enhance or disguise the flavor of this dish?" Even as an ardent sports fan, I'll confess that whatever is on ESPN has to be especially compelling to draw me away from *Diners, Drive-Ins, and Dives* on the Food Network. However, some time ago a personal friend who is an endocrinologist said, "Michael, you have to make a choice. The choice is whether or not you are going to be diabetic, because you are now pre-diabetic." It was a sobering moment. His counsel was simple: "You either find a new way to eat, or you will incur serious and life-changing consequences." Not wanting to face those consequences, I made a choice. It involved a certain amount of self-denial, which was not enjoyable. But it was based on a genuine sense of self-love. I now deny myself excessive carbs, which is not an easy thing for someone who so passionately enjoys cakes and pies and breads and pasta. I do so because I love my life and want to protect it. Therefore, I will take the requisite steps to do so.

Just as diet is essential to continued good health, so is reasonable exercise. A friend of mine says, "I consider elevators to be my enemy." You understand what he means. Something as simple as taking the stairs can enhance longevity and quality of life. The key is to find something that keeps the body moving. Jog, cycle, dance, do Yoga or Pilates, hike, lift free weights, join a gym, or just take long walks, which can involve solitude, meditation, or time spent playing with pets or visiting with friends. As a colleague often puts it, "Pick your passion." The simple act of moving the body on a regular basis keeps it strong, agile, and healthy and has a powerfully positive influence on our emotional well-being.

Paying proper attention to diet, reducing excessive intake of alcohol, avoiding tobacco products, saying no to drugs, getting reasonable exercise, and sleeping adequately are all expressions of appropriate self-love. Your body is the home of your spirit, and you dishonor that spirit (your essential self) if you disregard the needs of your body.

By the same token, self-love involves attending to the needs of your mind. Educators provide a valuable insight to all of us by calling graduation exercises "commencement." A commencement is a moment of beginning. Educators understand that receiving a degree does not mean one has completed the learning process, but rather that you are simply beginning it. The diploma one receives indicates that the graduate has been supplied with the necessary tools to embark on a lifetime of significant learning.

⁓

Years ago when I was a student at Duke University, I frequently saw an aged man sitting in library carrels with stacks of books and legal pads around him. He was always reading and taking notes as feverishly as if he were an undergrad preparing a term paper. When I asked a librarian about him, she replied, "He was a professor here for many years. He retired at age sixty-five, but twenty years later, he's still in the library every day. One day," she said, "I heard a young professor tell the older man that when he retires, he doesn't plan to spend his time in the library. And the old prof answered, 'Then how will you continue to learn?'"

The man had discovered a key to successful and meaningful living, and, I think, a key to not growing old regardless of how many years the body accumulates. If we keep our minds alert, active, and inquiring, we keep our lives vibrant and vital. Where we might say, "You're as young as you feel," we probably ought to say, "You are as young as you think!"

～

As one embarks on a pathway of reasonable self-love (designed to result in a lifetime of meaning and satisfaction), an appropriate question is: What are you doing to feed your mind? Just as I was challenged by a physician to pay special attention to what I feed my body, the same is necessary for us intellectually. Do we read? Do we keep up with current issues in politics, religion, literature, philosophy, sociology, science, and the arts? Whereas many of us enjoy the spirit and ambience of bookstores and libraries, it is undeniable that the Internet also provides amazing opportunities to expose ourselves to a vast array of information that resides at our fingertips. As is the case with physical exercise, so it is with the intellect: pick your passion and do something every day to exercise your mind. Otherwise, like any other muscle that is neglected, the mind weakens and the spirit feels tired and old.

4. SELF-LOVE INVOLVES AFFIRMING YOUR EMOTIONS.

From time to time people will say to me, "I am disturbed by these feelings that I have. They make me feel ashamed." I always answer, "Feelings are feelings. They are neither good nor bad. They simply are. What we do about feelings is quite another matter, and that's where our ethics and morals come into play. But you should never be ashamed of your feelings."

Too many of us are taught as children to repress. "Stop laughing!" "Stop crying!" "That's not funny!" "Keep it up, and I'll give you something to cry about!" Thus we are programmed to deny our feelings, which ultimately results in stunted emotional growth. Just the opposite is required for healthy self-actualization. Laugh frequently. Cry when you feel the emotion. The ancient Greeks were reflecting on more than just the craft of the stage when they emphasized the significance of the two emotional masks we humans wear. Embrace and explore what is going on inside you. Otherwise, the lens through which you see and interpret life will be clouded by all manners of unresolved issues.

∾

Some years ago, journalist Norman Cousins described his own bout with illness and the relief from pain and renewed strength he found through the power of laughter.[41] He suffered from numerous afflictions, serious illnesses for which doctors at that time said there were no known cures. He reported that immersing himself in humorous materials, including slapstick films such as those by the Marx Brothers, and allowing himself the luxury of unrestrained laughter brought about amazing results. Cousins claimed those results included everything from reduction of pain, which allowed uninterrupted sleep, to remission in his battle with what could have been a terminal illness. Scientists are not of one mind regarding how dramatic the effects of laughter may be on the human body. However, all scientists and physicians concur that laughter releases endorphins that possess definite and demonstrable positive effects on our physical well-being. And even if that were not the case, who can deny the positive impact of laughter on the human psyche?

∾

---

[41] Norman Cousins, *Anatomy of an Illness As Perceived by the Patient* (NY: W.W. Norton and Company, 1979).

We now have access to personalized radio stations on our mobile phones and laptops. Whether via Stitcher, Pandora, Spotify, or a host of others, we can request a style of entertainment we enjoy, and a computerized program will provide us an ongoing 24/7 menu of that precise style. On my Pandora account, for example, I have everything from Bach to the Beatles and from George Winston to Gloria Estefan. But my catalog of stations is also populated by other names, such as Jack Benny and Rita Rudner. I make certain that I can always hit "play" and listen to comedians. Often, the greater the level of stress in my life, the greater the benefit of listening to them and experiencing the healing properties of laughter. One of my sons is a therapist who sometimes says, "If people simply learned the value of laughing, the value of seeing life from a perspective informed by humor, then my client load would be considerably reduced." Learn the inherent psychological and physical benefits of humor. As a source of ancient wisdom rightfully reminds us, a happy heart is good medicine.[42]

Just as there is strength to be found in laughter, allowing ourselves the freedom to cry is also an undeniable method of maintaining emotional stability. A lifelong friend of mine works as a chaplain. He regularly counsels both individuals with serious illnesses and families facing crises. Some time ago he shared that, "About once every couple of weeks, I allow myself space to weep. Without doing so, I don't think that I could process all the pain I witness on a daily basis." Remember what was stated earlier: issues that are buried grow bigger. If those issues have to do with grief or sadness, repression can be physically damaging and emotionally deadly.

---

[42] Proverbs 17:22.

Think of the cleansing benefits of water as it flows around our bodies. Imagine sitting in a warm summer brook with the waters rushing around you or standing beneath an energizing shower following an hour's exercise. Think of the refreshing experience of allowing water to make you clean. That is also an inner reality and not just an external one. The water of tears purges our pain, allowing the residue of human hurt or disappointment to be washed out. An acquaintance who is a physician told me, "To stay healthy and properly manage stress, I encourage my patients to cry. Mature men and women need to understand that tears, far from being signs of weakness, often instead are signs of wisdom and stability."

Tears, obviously, are not just a release of painful emotions but can also be an expression of positive ones. Thus do we frequently hear or employ the phrase "tears of joy." A stirring piece of music often brings us to tears, as does witnessing wedding vows or deeds of heroism, or hearing stories of empathetic compassion, or being reunited with long-lost loved ones, or a host of other things. No matter how often I watch the movie *Field of Dreams*, I am always brought to tears by the closing scene when son and father at last play that long-awaited game of catch.

Self-love involves allowing yourself to feel what you feel and giving those emotions permission to be expressed. Laugh heartily. Weep when you feel like weeping. The benefits to mind, soul, and body are beyond calculation.

5. SELF-LOVE SHOULD OCCASIONALLY INVOLVE A BIT OF SELF-INDULGENCE.

In other words, from time to time, do not feel guilty about pampering yourself.

Buy tickets to a concert, even when there are more urgent places the price of those tickets could be spent. Get a massage. Take the vacation you have been putting off. Allow yourself to say, "This is something I want," and pursue it. If that is your constant pattern of living ("It's all about me, and the heck with what anyone else wants or needs!"), then you are 180 degrees away from the discipline of loving. But your love of neighbor should be seasoned with the awareness that you, also, are worthy of love, and your needs, as much as anyone else's, deserve attention. By coming to that awareness, you will be able to more fully love others in a meaningful way.

~~~

A highly-skilled therapist works in the same building that I do. He is both a colleague and a friend. Some time ago, we were discussing summer plans. He said that he and his wife were making a long-desired trip to France. I confessed that I was hoping to work in a little time here and there for R & R, but that finding the time was proving to be difficult.

He asked, "What do you love doing? What brings you peace?"

Numerous answers jumped to mind, but the primary one was, "I love going to the theater. It can be Broadway, off-Broadway, or off-off-Broadway. It can be a musical, a comedy, a serious drama, a monologue, or experimental theater. It really doesn't matter. For the two hours I'm in a theater, I forget everything except what I am watching. I always come away feeling refreshed and restored."

My friend replied, "Then take a little unsolicited professional advice from me. The best thing you can do for all the people who need and depend on you is to spend a little less time in the office and a little more time in the theater."

I chuckled.

But he looked me in the eye and continued, "If you do not take care of you, in time there will be no essential you left to take care of anyone else."

That was sound advice.

The wisdom of Joseph Campbell jumps to mind: "Follow your bliss."[43] What do you love to do? What brings you peace and fulfillment? What makes you smile? What gives you energy? What feeds your soul? What makes you feel refreshed and restored? Whatever it is, as my friend suggested to me, do more of it! For unless you take care of you, in time there will be no essential you left to take care of anyone else.

⌇⌇⌇

Years ago I was told of a nun who taught self-help and motivational seminars all across the country. Her clients were Roman Catholic and non-Catholic, religious and non-religious, male and female. People from every walk of life came to her because they needed to be reminded of the truth she offered. At the beginning of every seminar or conference she conducted, she had those in attendance do an exercise. They were all given a small pocket mirror. She had them stand, open the mirror, look into it, and say to the reflection, "You are truly beautiful."

[43] Joseph Campbell, *The Power of Myth* (NY: Doubleday, 1988), pp. 120, 149.

During the opening session, the exercise often brought laughter, comical (and sometimes self-deprecating) remarks, and a noticeable air of general discomfort. Throughout the seminar, however, she would emphasize and re-emphasize the value of having a healthy self-perception. She would use psychological data and human-interest anecdotes to reinforce the message that unless we appreciate ourselves properly, we are functionally unable to properly appreciate other people, daily experiences, or life itself. During times of group conversation, which occasionally included vivid and tearful confessions from individuals in attendance regarding the sources of their lack of self-esteem, she would respond with hugs and reassurance, always having them repeat the exercise from the opening session. At the final gathering of the seminar, she had everyone open their mirror, look into it, and say again the phrase with which they had begun. This time, however, there would be no laughter, no self-deprecation, and no lack of comfort. The participants would find themselves saying with a new air of understanding and self-worth, "You are truly beautiful." Finally being able to confess that truth about their own lives, they were liberated to see and affirm the inherent beauty in others. Put another way, by loving themselves they were empowered to also love their neighbors and their world.

If we are to establish the discipline of loving as the core active principle of life—and thereby find a meaning in life that cannot be located through any other discipline—inevitably we must learn and practice the art of self-love. Without that, any other love we experience or express will be less than whole.

TEN

A SPIRITUAL
ENDEAVOR

Consider the following list of statements, taken from the holy writings of the world's great faiths:

- "And if thine eye be turned towards justice, choose thou for thy neighbor that which thou choosest for thyself." (Bahá'í)

- "Hurt not others in ways you yourself would find hurtful." (Buddhism)

- "In everything do to others as you would have them do to you; for this is the law and the prophets." (Christianity)

- "Do not unto others what you do not want them to do to you." (Confucianism)

- "This is the sum of duty: do naught unto others which would cause you pain if done to you." (Hinduism)

- "Not one of you is a believer until he loves for his brother what he loves for himself." (Islam)

- "A man should wander about treating all creatures as he himself would be treated." (Jainism)

- "What is hateful to you, do not to your neighbor; that is the whole truth of the Torah; all the rest is commentary." (Judaism)

- "Respect for all life is the foundation." (Native American)

- "Treat others as thou wouldst be treated thyself." (Sikhism)

- "Regard your neighbor's gain as your own gain and your neighbor's loss as your own loss." (Taoism)

- "That nature alone is good which refrains from doing unto another whatsoever is not good for itself." (Zoroastrianism)

All those statements[44] are variations of what we call *the Golden Rule*, a rule accepted and proclaimed by spiritual institutions and religious leaders of the world across the ages. Whatever the faith, all profess in their sacred writings that love of neighbor as of self is the universally affirmed code of human conduct. And were that one standard observed in relationships, whether personal, institutional, or international (especially among those who claim to be adherents of faith), then we would live in a world free of crime, abuse, victimization of the vulnerable, poverty, and war.

---

[44] from The Tanenbaum Center, NY, NY, www.tanenbaum.org.

Any consideration of the theme of spirituality seems to quickly evoke a voice that asks, "But what of those who have no belief system? Are you saying they cannot fully realize the power of love, and, thus, of joyful living?" To that I have two separate answers. The first is this: "You are referring to religion, but I was speaking of spirituality." (At the close of the chapter, we will explore the difference, striving for an understanding of what it means to be a spiritual person. Up until that point, of course, employment of the term "spiritual" will continue, since the disciplines of theology and spirituality inevitably overlap.)

My second answer, however, does deal with religion. That is because of the overlap just noted. Religion and spirituality are linked in so profound a way that it is difficult to talk of the latter without carefully considering the former. So my religious answer to the question "What of those who have no belief?" is, "I've never really met an atheist." To be sure, I have met many who claim to be such, but I've never known a person whose claim completely stands up. The simple fact is that none of us can know that which we can not know. So just as no person can prove by empirical data that God exists, neither can anyone conclusively prove that God is nonexistent. At best, many people are simply agnostics who lean in one direction or the other.

The word "atheist" means "one without belief" (or "without theism"). Have you ever truly met a person who did not believe in or commit to something with a greater devotion than to everything else? The simple truth is that whatever we value most in life becomes our god. We believe in whatever that something is with a passion that is, in fact, reverent. Therefore, essentially there is not so much a-theism as there is simply redefined theism. We all worship something. For some folks, the object of worship is self. For others, possessions. For some, sexuality. For others, nature. For some, humanism. For others, hedonism. For some, a traditional understanding of God as revealed through a sacred text. For others, a traditional understanding of God as revealed through a different sacred text, which makes their tradition of God very much unlike someone else's. But we all elevate something or someone to a central psychological or spiritual pedestal. We all have a god of some sort.

Whatever name we attach to it, most people, in fact, believe in a divine power beyond self, even beyond that which can be seen and proved in temporal ways. Some call that power God, others Allah, others Yahweh, others Fate, or Divine Intelligence, or Spirit, or Mother, or Father, or Source, or Creative Energy, or Divine Insight, or Ground of all Being,[45] or Guided Intuition, or a host of other titles up to and including "the Force" (as in "May the Force be with you").[46] The names are plentiful, but the concept remains the same: there is something (or someone) beyond us that endows our lives with meaning and dignity. And authentic living can be attained through encounter with and inspiration from that power.

If that power does, indeed, encounter and inspire us, then something of it is obviously within us. And if it is within us, undeniably therefore it is also within others. A friend of mine lost two brothers in the tragic AIDS epidemic of the late twentieth century. One of the brothers (my friend's

---

[45] A theological euphemism for God made famous by Paul Tillich.

[46] A line frequently used in all *Star Wars* movies, but first spoken in the original movie by the character of General Dodonna. *Star Wars*. Dir. George Lucas. 20th Century Fox, 1977.

twin) spent much of his life on a spiritual quest. Toward the end, he said, "I've seen the face of God, and it is my own." That is an example of incarnational theology—experiencing the reality of God through human expression. Historically that is how God has been most helpfully understood. So, if God is in me, then God is in you. If God is in you, then God is in me. Thus, to express love to a human "other" is to express love to the Divine Other. Consider again teachings of various sacred texts and how they concur regarding love of neighbor:

- "Allah commands justice, the doing of good and giving to kith and kin, and He forbids all indecent deeds and evil and transgression; He instructs you that you may remember this."[47]

- "What does the Lord require of you but to do justice, to love mercy, and to walk humbly with your God?"[48]

- "This is my commandment, that you love one another as I have loved you."[49]

In each of those quotes, it is clear that the love we share with another human being becomes an act of reverence, an acknowledgment of a spark of the Divine within our neighbors.

In the same fashion, to love one's self is to love the Spirit of the Divine that exists within us. Consider the sad

---

[47] Quran 16:90.

[48] Micah 6:8.

[49] John 15:12.

lesson of Rev. Arthur Dimmesdale[50] in *The Scarlet Letter* who, though proclaiming an allegiance to a God of grace, was unable to express grace to others or appropriate it for himself. Thus did a messenger of "good news of great joy"[51] live a tortured life primarily because he was never able to forgive and love himself. How is it possible to live a life of self-loathing if we believe that the Spirit of the Divine is within us? Certainly, we may regret past decisions that cannot be amended. But, as noted previously, we learn lessons from the past in order to build a healthier future. To hate one's self is to disdain the greater Spirit that resides within one's self.

All the world's great faiths affirm the same wisdom— that we are called to practice love. On the one hand, we are called to love others, acknowledging that doing so reveals a respect for the Higher Power that dwells within neighbor. On the other hand, we are called to appropriately love self, acknowledging that the Divine chose to take up residence within our hearts and souls and flesh and bones. Love and spirituality are therefore virtually inseparable. The inherent power of spirituality is available to those who give themselves to the practice of loving. In fact, it is inescapable. Whatever your faith system may be, loving emerges from the deepest and purest place in the human spirit. When you love, you are a spiritual person.

Furthermore, if God is—not just "is in you" or "is in me," but simply "is"—then we can experience Divine Reality (the source of love and, therefore, of life) in numerous ways. Some are cerebral and meditative. Others

---

[50] From Nathaniel Hawthorne's *The Scarlet Letter* (Boston: Ticknor and Fields, 1850).

[51] Luke 2:10.

are active. But what we learned as children is probably still as deep and wise as any other lessons we've been taught about the Divine. When told, "God is love," someone painted the clearest picture of Ultimate Reality that one can see. Theologies differ widely about a host of dogmatic positions and philosophies. But virtually all faith systems confess the fundamental truth of this statement. This much I know for certain: God really is love. Therefore, we come to know God by immersing ourselves in the daily discipline of loving. And, conversely, we come to understand the infinite power of love, which is the one true secret to happiness, by knowing more and more about whatever we understand God to be.

So let's take a look at a few suggestions regarding how we can develop and deepen our personal spirituality. Remember, doing so is a sure avenue to discovering the unshakable foundation of love upon which all other desirable virtues (such as peace, hope, self-worth, relationship, meaning, and happiness) are located. How does one go about nurturing the spiritual side of life?

1. PRACTICE THE ART OF MEDITATION.

This requires, first and foremost, the discipline of silence. No cell phones nearby. No TVs or CD players operating (although it can be helpful to have some soft, spa-like music playing in the background, much like that which might be played when receiving a therapeutic massage, just not at high volume). No laptops or iPads in the room. Light a candle. Sit quietly in a relaxed physical posture, whether a yoga position or simply in a chair, breathing deeply, with both feet on the floor. Focus on silence and stillness.

Remember the wisdom from Hebrew scripture: "Be still, and know that I am God."[52]

Meditation is the art of allowing the universe to come to us, not taking our issues to the universe. It is pausing in divine presence with no other agenda than to be and, perhaps, to hear. I have found that mental imaging is important, but it is best if the image comes to us rather than our working to create one. A spiritual director coached me to "push all thoughts and issues out of your mind for now, and see God as God is to you." That is not an easy task when initially attempted, but it becomes easier when practiced with intentional stillness and waiting. At last, an image came to me that I had in no way anticipated. It was the image of a clear night with reflections of starlight shimmering off a glassy

lake. I saw myself cradled in loving arms. That was the image of God that was within my subconscious and, through personal meditation, at last managed to reach me in conscious moments. God was loving arms that cradled and comforted me, as a child held in the safety of a mother's embrace. In time, it was easier and easier to access that image when practicing meditation. And, safe within that image, I began to experience spiritual and emotional growth that my hectic, hurried, weary, and worried self had not previously allowed to emerge.

Simply sitting and focusing on an image, word, or even a sound (as in a Hindu mantra) enables you to be open to a wisdom that our busy-ness too often shuts out. Medical experiments likewise suggest that the practice of meditation reduces blood pressure and heart rate. In other words, the benefits are both spiritual and physical. So what does that

---

[52] Ps. 46:10.

tell us? It tells you and me that meditation is a source of personal peace. When we come to a place of peace, we come to a place where grasping and understanding the essence of love (and therefore, the essence of life) is a possibility. At the very least, meditation is a way to center in divine presence (the love of God) that brings demonstrable benefits to the one who meditates.

2. ADD THE PRACTICE OF PRAYER TO THE DISCIPLINE OF MEDITATION.

The two practices are similar but not necessarily synonymous. Prayer, at its best, is an act of listening, much like meditation. It is also, however, an act of communicating that which we hold deepest within us to a power whom we trust to have our best interests at heart. So it is both listening and speaking. Prayer is a kind of conversation between the holy and the mortal.

A wise theologian provided me with helpful advice many years ago. He said, "Forget all the formal prayers you heard in churches growing up. Throw out words like 'Thee' and 'Thou' and 'Thine.' Instead, talk to God like you would speak to your best friend who is seated across the table from you with a cup of coffee." With that in mind, prayer was transformed for me from a liturgical ritual to a personal encounter.

"Talk to God like you would speak to your best friend who is seated across the table from you with a cup of coffee." Express fear, anger, frustration, confusion, joy, hope ... whatever abides deep within you. Say it out loud, as if a best friend were listening. And imagine that friend as someone who will never judge you for what you feel, but will love you fully and freely no matter what. Once that prayer posture is attained, we are able to give voice to things from the depths of our emotions, no holds barred. The psychological beauty of that is that sometimes things emerge that we had repressed, things we did not know were even within us at all. In therapy sessions with counselors, clients often confess, "I can't believe I just said that. I cannot believe those words crossed my lips. Where did that come from?" Every competent counselor will answer, "Where do you think it came from? And what do you think is the source of what you just expressed?" In that moment, when words gush forth that catch you by surprise, you gain valuable self-insight. That can also happen in prayer once a person becomes comfortable with the practice. We open ourselves up to a flow of consciousness that originates in the subconscious. When we move from liturgical formality to honest conversation, we sometimes pause mid-prayer and confess, "I can't believe I just said that. Where did that come from?" And part of the power of prayer becomes the next step of vigilant introspection and self-discovery.

When one decides to embark upon the lifelong journey of love, it is a healthy and helpful practice to periodically compose prayer questions. Addressing God in whatever terms or images seem most authentic to you, ask aloud, "Why am I having trouble loving in this situation?" "Why is it challenging to love that particular person?" "Why do I labor so much with a sense of guilt or remorse?" "Why is it almost impossible for me to forgive him or her?" The initial question can be followed by another, beginning with the phrase, "Do you think it is because …?" In that moment, be prepared to hear self-revelatory statements that may surprise you. "I can't believe I just said that. Where did that come from?" It comes from a place of honesty that seeks wholeness, a spiritual place that recognizes an issue standing between you and your longing to be made whole. It is impossible to be a complete (satisfied, at peace, authentic, happy) human being unless we at last live our lives practicing the daily discipline of love. Honest prayer is a tremendously effective tool in helping us realize where our own personal roadblocks are, as well as realizing that there is a source of resolution at our disposal.

3. PRACTICE REGULAR JOURNALING.

That may be one of the most important disciplines available to us in the search to know the Divine Other (especially to witness the intersection of that Other in our own lives).

A minister with whom I am acquainted lost her husband when their daughter was six years old. My acquaintance said she was determined not to let that loss impair her daughter's outlook on life. So the mother came up with an idea. She located a large, clear jar. She and her child created a paper mâché covering to paste on the outside. On the covering, the mom had her daughter paint the words, "Blessings Jar."

Each night before bed, mom and daughter would review the events of the day, and mom had a rule: "We will write down one good thing that happened to you today." Often the child argued that there were no good things to write. "My teacher is mean." "The cafeteria lunch was terrible." "My friends weren't nice to me." "It rained." But mom would always persist, "No, there had to be at least one good thing that you can remember, however small it might have been and however awful you think your day was." Finally the child (often reluctantly) would come up with a single idea. Together they would write it down and place it in the Blessings Jar. On the last night of every month, mother and daughter together would empty the jar onto the bed and read each day's entry, reminding her child of the wealth of good things that had happened to her over the course of a single month and of the fact that something good occurs every day. "I want to program my daughter to understand," the mother told me, "that though life is sometimes difficult and unfair, amid all that we receive daily blessings."

That child's experience was the first step into the practice of journaling. I regularly counsel people who are interested in spiritual disciplines to quietly review the events of each day before going to sleep. Write down your reflections. Record where you experienced serendipities, unexpected gestures of friendship, random acts of kindness, unanticipated compliments, or brief evidences of the reality of God. Note where you did things well, or lessons you learned from mistakes or errors. Especially make certain each night to include positive experiences from the day. Then at the end of each month, read back through the journal. That practice dramatically impacts our worldview, helping us become increasingly aware of goodness and grace and possibilities and potential and blessings and beauties and glasses half full. It also causes us to reflect on the source of those blessings, thus deepening our sense of connectedness to that which is beyond us.

4. LIVE THE SPIRITUAL LIFE IN COMMUNITY WITH OTHERS.

Meditation and prayer are personal experiences. Often the presence of others detracts from the fullness of those particular moments. However, there are other moments that cry out for community. Worship, theological exploration, and shared service all become exponentially stronger when done in concert with other individuals of a similar faith commitment.

I can think about God alone, but I cannot create a private liturgy that feels complete. I cannot baptize myself. I can consider what words like "faith," "sacrament," or "grace" mean, but I cannot learn what they have meant in a biblical, theological, or historical context without a teacher. Furthermore, my understanding of any theological concept deepens when discussed within a circle of others also seeking increased understanding. I can make a donation to a helping agency, and it may assist some people in a minimal or moderate way. But when my contribution is combined with the gifts of hundreds or thousands of others, a cumulative impact can be made that transcends what any one individual can make alone. I can do a bit of painting or carpentry solo, but it takes a group working together to erect a Habitat house.

There are certain experiences on the spiritual journey that are made stronger when lived out within a community.

5. SPEND TIME READING SACRED TEXTS.

Whether that text is the Quran, the Hebrew Scriptures, the New Testament, the writings of Confucius, or any of a number of others, one thing is almost certain: careful study of the text will reveal the priority of loving. All the world's great faiths affirm that. Sometimes we hijack faith systems and turn them ugly, using them to justify all sorts of inhumane practices (history is littered with such examples, from the Crusades to the current exploits of al-Qaeda and ISIS). We even attach bizarre titles like "holy war." But any honest exploration of sacred writings shows that "faith" and "love" are two sides of one coin. You cannot be a person of faith and at the same time be motivated by hatred, anger, prejudice, or revenge. Faith calls for all its practitioners to love. There is simply no getting around that. "If someone says he loves God but hates his brother or sister, he is a liar. For you cannot love God, whom you have not seen, if you hate people, whom you have seen."[53] The study of sacred books encourages all serious readers to embrace the philosophy of active loving and everything it involves.

6. ALLOW FOR THE POSSIBILITY OF THEOLOGICAL ASCENT.

Put more simply, don't ever assume you know enough, let alone all there is to know, about your concept of God and what that can potentially mean for the human journey. Be open to and actively seek deeper insights and more spiritually-based perspectives.

Those farthest along the journey come to simple and often childlike places. If one explores the nature of God long and carefully enough, he or she winds up where, as previously noted, we all were as children. We arrive at a genuine understanding that God really is love, after all. And, if we are created in God's image, then our true nature is to be lovers. Isn't it intriguing that we mature into childhood? The greater our spiritual insights, the more we at last come to own what we were told as toddlers. The greatest power in the universe is the nature of its creative force: love! And as

---

[53] I John 4:20.

part of Creation, we were made to experience and express that attribute. You and I were created to put love into practice. And most of our personal unhappiness is rooted in a failure to understand the purpose of our creation and/or a reluctance to live up to it.

Deductive reasoning makes it simple: if God is love, and if God is a part of me, then I am love in action! By accepting the first two premises of that statement, the conclusion becomes obvious and irrefutable. Someone or something made you and me for the pure purpose of loving. And when we live into that purpose, we finally become happy and whole. It really is that simple.

7. BELIEVING IN THE HOLY IS NOT ENOUGH UNTIL WE ACT ON WHAT WE BELIEVE.

In other words: When your belief system deepens, do something about it. Let meditation, prayer, and theological inquiry lead to actions such as service, the stewardship of nature, advocacy, forgiveness, seeing the world in a more positive perspective, practicing thankfulness, or advocating for the abused or the vulnerable. If faith informs us, it invariably informs us of the mandate to love. If we take spirituality seriously, we respond to that mandate.

⌇

Years ago I lived in a city with a wonderful automobile museum. It had everything from original Model T Fords (the ones for which Henry Ford used discarded milk crates to build the floorboards) to vintage Aston Martins, Bentleys, and Rolls-Royces. There were cars that had burst onto the scene and disappeared just as quickly, like Edsels and DeLoreans. When my sons, Adam and Zachary, were in elementary school, we toured the museum together.

Midway through our first tour, Zachary (then a first-grader) turned to me and asked, "Dad, who drives these cars?"

I answered, "No one."

My response obviously left him seriously puzzled. Even a first-grader knows that a car cannot magically drive itself unless its name is Herbie.

I continued, "Son, these cars are not for driving. They are for display only. No one takes them on the road. They always stay right here in the museum."

The concept eluded him altogether. He pondered for a moment and then asked, "But, Dad, why be a car if you never drive?"

Good question.

If a person takes spirituality seriously, eventually the questions emerge:

- You have a belief, so what?

- What are you going to do about it?

- How will your belief system inform or transform your decision-making, actions, and relationships?

In short, if you want to be a car, then when do you plan on driving?

~~~

Sometimes the actions we take will be nothing short of dramatic. We extend an olive branch to someone who deliberately or maliciously hurt us. We march on city hall. We give our time or financial resources to a cause that makes life better for people. We get behind the wheel and drive the car.

A successful friend who manages a multimillion-dollar-per-year company spent a week volunteering at a food pantry. For a full week, he packaged meals to be delivered to people who were homebound due to illness or injury. He also served meals to homeless and marginally-housed individuals and to families who came into the facility. It was polemically opposite to all that he ordinarily does with his time. At week's end he was absolutely jubilant, filled with an energy I had not seen in him before. He, in fact, could not adequately interpret the feelings that welled up in him and, indeed, spilled over. He said to me, "This was such menial and difficult work. Why on earth do I feel so good?" I answered, "You feel good because for a week you lived up to your birthright. You actually did what you were created to do. For a full week, everything you did was an act of love. So, for a full week you were authentically alive."

On the other hand, sometimes our actions are more subtle than dramatic but are still impactful. In fact, the mere determination to do no harm can be an act of loving that reflects a mature spirituality.

What if a person simply made the following commitment: "I resolve not to intentionally harm anyone anymore"? Nothing other than that. Not "I will save the world." Not "I will re-configure the offensive or oppressive systems of a city's government." Not "I will champion a cause." Not even "I will offer to bury the hatchet with someone with whom I have been at odds," or "I will extend an olive branch to someone who hurt me." What if we simply made the commitment not to intentionally harm anyone anymore? That one simple declaration places a person squarely on the side of love and in the camp of whatever you define God to be. And it also adds immeasurably to the quality of life, both in the world and in the heart of the individual making the commitment.

~~~

Let's return to a question with which this chapter began: "Is there a difference between spirituality and religion?" The answer, of course, is "Yes." A religion is a belief system embraced by numerous people who become adherents of a particular theology and a way of observing it (ritualizing and practicing the belief system). It possesses an identifiable religious history, the affirmation of sainted or special people within that history, lexicons for describing faith issues, predictable methods of worship, and formalized protocols for becoming part of and maintaining membership within the group. Spirituality, on the other hand, is not so formalized, nor is it necessarily institutionalized. A spiritual person is an individual of depth and insight that goes beyond the obvious and beneath the superficial. He or she is a person who does not confuse information with wisdom, or even wisdom with Truth.

A spiritual person is committed to soul as much as to life and, in fact, believes that one's life cannot properly be understood or appreciated without attention to the care of one's soul. By "soul," the spiritual person means "essence." Who or what are you essentially, deep in your heart, in your original or hidden self? My conviction is that you and I are entities in search of love—in search of experiencing it and also expressing it. That is our essential nature. That is the DNA of our souls. We were created for the pure purpose of love. Along our journey, a host of unenlightened influences pressure us to follow lesser paths. And none of those paths ever lead to joy.

Consider, for example, the sex-for-sale industry. It is a multibillion-dollar industry that is directly related to a long litany of dark and dehumanizing issues: trafficking, forced prostitution, pimps, kidnapping, slavery, pornography, organized crime, divorce or the dissolution of primary monogamous relationships, disease, death, and the list goes on and on. Or consider relational infidelity. Despite the adrenaline rush (or denial of aging) that is ordinarily part of an initial flirtation, the ultimate outcomes can be just as demoralizing as was the case with the preceding topic and can include, but are not limited to: shame, guilt, pain inflicted upon people who trusted, divorce or the dissolution of primary monogamous relationships, disease, and so on. In each case, a superficial hunger is fed that does not (and usually cannot) attend to the deeper hunger that exists. The superficial need that is addressed is sexuality, or physical connection, or a momentary break from loneliness or isolation. The method of meeting that need is sensual (not spiritual) and fleeting. In short, once the encounter is concluded, the need beneath the need remains unattended. And what is "the need beneath the need" that leads individuals to sexual (but not spiritual) encounters? It is the desire for intimacy. The desire to know and be known, to love and be loved. Joni Mitchell expresses it beautifully in one of her songs: "Love is touching souls."[54] And that cannot be done with rented strangers, for their

---

[54] Joni Mitchell, "A Case of You," from the album *Blue* (Reprise Records, 1971).

souls are not made available for the client to touch nor are they interested in touching the soul of the client. Nor can it be done in relationships built upon dishonesty, which have to be hidden from public view. Sexuality and spirituality are keenly related human experiences. And the sexual moment, replete with all its physical ecstasy, is enhanced when not only bodies touch but also, in the process, "love is touching souls."

Or consider the spirituality of one's profession, which might possibly also be called "the spirituality of economics." Do we do what we do only to make money? The value of earning is by no means a negative thing, as long as said earning symbolizes something deeper. There's a profound distinction between saying, "I make

a lot of money," and saying, "I make a lot of difference." Or to quote the phrase we often hear, "There is a wide gap between making a living and making a life." Income is important and may give a person a partial view of his or her accomplishments in a particular professional discipline. Income in and of itself, however, is never more than a means to an end. Income cannot buy intellect or sophistication or an artistic spirit or inner peace or true friends or ultimate joy. It may purchase lovely garments to cover a person's exterior, but it cannot touch what lies beneath the skin.

Some who have lost touch with their primary purpose— that we are created for love—will, of their own confusion, try to convince others that money is a desired end. That philosophy of life begs all sorts of crucial questions, not the least of which are:

- How did you make your money?

- What lines of ethics are you willing to transgress to make more?

- How do you use your resources? For the common good or simply for your own personal purposes?

- Do you realize the inherent value of those who have changed the world but did not possess the material resources that you would deify? Put another way, are you able to see the incredible contributions of people like Mother Teresa, Albert Schweitzer, or Gandhi, who raised the world's understanding of the meaning of life but had very little of the world's treasures to show for it?

Earning money is neither inherently positive nor negative. What makes it either depends on how we earn it and what we subsequently do with it. Make a mental list of the truly happiest people you know. My guess is that they will share the common quality of investing themselves in making the world a better place for other people. Some are folks of considerable financial means, but they see those resources, at least to a reasonable extent, as tools for helping those who cannot help themselves and for supporting causes that strengthen the world around them. Plus, there is for them an insight that goes much deeper than the shallowness of greed or consumerism. They possess a spirituality of economics.

Does the artist paint, sculpt, or compose for the want of fame or fortune? Just as there is a spiritual dimension of such things as sexuality and economics, there's also a deeply spiritual side of the arts. Read the great poetry of the centuries. Across the years, the verses that have lingered and possessed the power to challenge and transform minds have been poems that are deeply spiritual. That does not mean they regularly dealt with religious themes, but they dealt with essential themes, with the raw stuff of the soul, and with Truth, or else with humanity's hunger for it.

∽∾

A friend of mine works for an agency that represents musical artists. He has a stable and profitable job, and he is quite talented at it. But he originally came to the city to be a singer. Ultimately, he represents musicians because he loves music. From time to time on his way home from eight hours of work in a Manhattan office, he will take off his coat and tie, find a corner on a subway platform, and begin to sing. He sings Broadway show tunes, music from the Great American Songbook, from Cole Porter and the Gershwins, as people hurry by. Many hardly notice he is there. Others pause and listen before boarding their trains. But for my friend, it is not about winning the applause of an adoring audience. It is about the music. Music is the deepest expression of his soul. As he puts it, "Occasionally I sing because I must sing. The music demands my voice. And when I give in to that demand, I am alive!"

∽∾

True artists express for the pure love of the art. However left-brained a person may be, there is a longing from the right side that calls for articulation. Draw the picture, write the short story, play the instrument, sing the song for the pure love of expressing what demands to be expressed. In so doing your spirituality is enhanced, and you experience a kind of love that underscores and illumines the purpose of your existence.

We could go on and on with this, but the point is clear. Pick a topic. It can become mundane or majestic depending on whether or not we allow it to be a spiritual experience. In virtually any field or discipline of life, we can stay at the surface and deal with superficial (even mechanical) matters, or we can dive deeper and deal with essence and reality. I can see in beekeeping simply a way to make honey or to sell a product. Or I can see those as mere components of a greater endeavor. What if beekeeping helps me understand a form of life that unfolds and works before my eyes? What if it helps me understand the mystery of nature as creatures move from instinct and affect a literal transformation of substance? And thus, what if it moves me to a deep awareness that I am one with the process and can replicate it, at least, in emotional ways? You see the difference. It's a matter of perception and how we view things either from a pedantic place or spiritual place. It is the difference between perceiving notes or hearing music, between reading words or experiencing poetry, between existing and living. To live is to embrace one's spirituality, whether that is in a religious sense or in a sense of bringing one's soul to the ordinary experiences of life whereby they become extraordinary.

Ultimately, the essence of God, however you define that term, is love. And the pure purpose of one's life, of one's soul or essence, is to experience and express love. What the world needs now is what it has always needed, and what you and I need as well. We need to be loved and to pass that love along. That is our spiritual calling. That is our highest purpose. That is our ultimate destiny. That is our path to an inner joy that nothing else can give and, once found, nothing else can destroy.

Love is the highway that leads to happiness. It often has steep hills to climb. It possesses twists and turns that have to be carefully navigated. But if happiness is your desired destination, love is the only road that will get you there.

GOING FORTH

"Life is what you make it." I've heard that since my youth. For a long while, I dismissed it as simplistic. Life throws things our way that we neither anticipate nor desire. Were we given the chance to make life what we want it to be, we would construct it differently. We would all be rich, beautiful, and healthy.

Over time, however, I've come to realize the wisdom of that which I once dismissed. The statement is not so simple or shallow as it initially seemed. I do have the freedom to make something special of my life. Certainly there are parameters, but within them I have choices. And those choices include finding happiness and sharing it with others, making a difference in the world around me, discovering a sense of meaning and purpose, improving relationships, reducing stress, and knowing that my life counts for something. All that and more is mine by making the choice to base my life on the principle of active loving.

In this book I have sought to provide an understanding of what that means. Yes, this approach to life makes demands

LOVE IS THE WAY

of us. But the returns far exceed the investments required. As I urged at the beginning of this book: find love, find life! If the eventual return is authentic life, the real deal, then it is more than worth the effort required to find it.

As I look back across the span of my life, the moments that stand out most positively all had to do with love. I recall my mom sitting in a rocking chair beside my bed when I was sick as a child. She would sing and reassure me that I was on the mend. Her very presence made me less afraid and, therefore, assisted in the healing process. She sat up late at night and missed sleep in order to give me the gift of love.

∽

I recall my dad, a broadcast journalist and instructor of public speaking, who taught me how to deliver a speech. He taught me how to breathe, how to maintain eye contact with the audience while glancing at notes, how to segue from point to point, and even how to use a stage whisper. Most of all, he taught me that someone believed in me. He gave me the gift of love.

I recall how it felt the first time I held my babies in my arms. They did not know me. There was nothing they could do for me. But from the first moment I held them, I knew that I had been introduced to human beings I would be willing to die for, and that made me suddenly feel all the more alive. I remember the sound of their childhood voices when they called me "Daddy" and the touch of their chubby preschool hands gripping my own as we crossed the street. Years have passed and even still, they've given (and continue to give) me the gift of love.

208

I remember boyhood teachers, coaches, and pastors who made me feel noticed and special. They affirmed within me gifts that I didn't even know I had. They encouraged me, mentored me, and did it all with exceeding patience. To a great extent, I wanted to achieve in order to make them proud of me. Their fingerprints remain on my life. They gave me the gift of love.

~~~

At night when I come home from tiring or trying days, I have a wife who consistently asks, "How was your day?" Most of the time my responses are positive because I find that living by the principle of active loving makes for a happy life. Even so, there are stresses or disappointments inherent in living. I share them with her and find strength and comfort in her caring spirit. We laugh together and dream together. My life is better because she is part of it. She gives me the gift of love.

Countless friends are sources of light amid the world's shadows. One in particular comes to mind. During a singularly trying season some years ago, he and I would have lunch together once a week. He had a mantra that he shared with me at each meal: "If you want to talk, I'll listen. If you prefer not to, I'll just sit with you in silence. If you want to laugh, I'll tell a joke. If you feel like crying, we will cry together." In his presence, I found strength to keep moving forward, week by week. He gave me the gift of love.

My love of sports, my love of literature, my love of theater, my love of nature, my love of music, and my love of faith have all enriched my life in immeasurable ways. Reflecting back on life to this point, it is clear that the experience of loving—whatever the source or whatever the object—is what enriches my life. Love turns existing into living!

So I want to conclude this work by simply recommending to you what I am certain beyond any question can make all the difference in your world. I know because it has made and continues to make all the difference in mine. We are born into this life without a penny in our pockets. We will exit the same way. Therefore, what matters is not what we accumulate, but what we become. Your life will be happy to the extent that you become a practitioner of love—a lover of people, a lover of self, a lover of life.

As I think about the readers who have journeyed with me through this book, I am certain of two things. First, you are profoundly different from one another. You work at different jobs, live in different places, are of different ethnic backgrounds, have different tastes in food, listen to different music, vote for different candidates, cheer for different athletic teams, watch different movies, and have different perspectives on countless issues. Your loves and your interests are unique to you. The second thing of which I'm convinced is that in spite of our differences, we all have one thing in common: time. We are all given twenty-four hours per day, one hundred and sixty-eight hours per week, no more, no less. And the quality of our lives depends on what we do with the time at our disposal while we still have it.

Will we make our time meaningful, transformative, and happy? Will we do more than just punch clocks or take up space? What will we do with our lives? What will we make of the time we have?

In order to make the absolute most of life (finding joy, peace, purpose, and health in the process), there is no alternative to the daily discipline of active loving. Remember the question posed earlier in this work: "Is this the loving thing to say or do?" If that one criterion is employed before we make decisions, it will change the nature of living for us. Life will become what we make it, and we will make it meaningful and happy. What will you make of the time you have while you have it?

The choice is yours. I hope you will find life by loving. Ultimately it's the only way life can be found. Make the most of the time that is yours. Seize life. Practice love. Be happy.

-Michael B. Brown

ACKNOWLEDGEMENTS

With special thanks to …

Honoree Corder for inspiration and guidance

Jeffrey Hayzlett for encouragement and counsel

Alison Haile for making everything else happen once the words were on paper

and Page for never letting me get too busy to remember what my real business is

ABOUT THE AUTHOR

DR. MICHAEL B. BROWN is an author, motivational speaker, adjunct professor, and for ten years was Senior Minister at Marble Collegiate Church in New York City, America's oldest existing Protestant congregation (served for many years by Norman Vincent Peale who wrote the international best seller, *The Power Of Positive Thinking*). All across America in civic arenas, at corporate events, on college and university campuses, and for Chautauqua Institutes, Dr. Brown carries the mantle of positivity to audiences of all ages, teaching a proven approach to discovering meaning, healthy relationships, and joy in life.

A native North Carolinian, Michael Brown graduated from High Point University, earned a Masters degree from

Duke University, and received Doctoral degrees from both Drew University and Pfeiffer University. He is the author of numerous books and also contributes regularly to *The Huffington Post* and *Thrive Global.*

Dr. Brown has been featured in four ABC-TV specials, one PBS special, and has another scheduled for ABC in 2018. He is a member of the National Speakers Association (NSA) and has also been a guest on MSNBC, Fox News, and NET TV. He is a frequent speaker on the international radio program *Day1*, and has been a featured guest on a variety of network radio and Sirius programs (including shows hosted by Timothy Cardinal Dolan, Jeffrey Hayzlett, Mike Stoller, Rabbi Joe Potasnik, and Laura Smith on "Saturday Café").

Dr. Brown always designs his message of "practical positivity" to meet the specific needs of the particular audience he addresses, using humor and anecdotes to describe a philosophy of life assured to bring meaning, joy, and hope to those who practice it. Among the topics he often explores are:

- Four Paths to a Meaningful Life
- Prescription for Happiness
- Think Your Way to a Brand New You
- Ages and Stages: The Life Journey
- Free to be Whole: The Forgiveness Factor
- Pulling Your Own Strings
- Dreaming the Right Dreams (And Making Them Come True)

Whatever your institution's agenda may be, Michael Brown will be happy to work with you in developing the ideal presentation to meet your goals.

89880827R00131

Made in the USA
San Bernardino, CA
02 October 2018